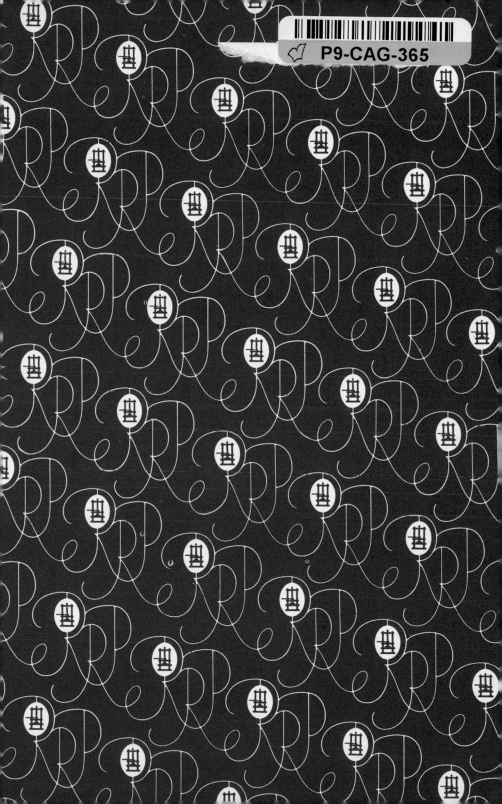

# TURN YOURSELF ON:
Goal Planning for Success

# TURN YOURSELF ON:

Goal Planning for Success

ROBERT E. LINNEMAN, PH.D.

RICHARDS ROSEN PRESS, INC., NEW YORK, N.Y. 10010

To worthwhile goals:
Annabelle, Danny,
Kurt, and of course,
Bert, who started me
in the right direction.

*Standard Book Number: 8239–0184–x*
*Library of Congress Catalog Card Number: 77–93292*

Published in 1970 by Richards Rosen Press, Inc.
29 East 21st Street, New York City, N.Y. 10010

*Copyright 1970 by Robert E. Linneman*

*FIRST EDITION*

*Manufactured in the United States of America*

## About the Author

Robert E. Linneman is an Associate Professor at Temple University, teaching courses in Marketing Management at the undergraduate and graduate levels. No "ivy tower isolate," Dr. Linneman is a living contradiction to the cliché, "Those who can't do, teach." He has served as a consultant to a number of firms in various types of industries, such as publishing, pharmaceuticals, regional development associations, public utilities, electronic data processing, and banks, to name but a few. As a consultant, Dr. Linneman has often been directly involved in setting goals and developing plans for organizations.

While serving in the dual capacity of consultant and professor, he began to realize that students were lacking a systematic method of planning for their lives. They needed a planning procedure similar to that used by industry. By following such a systematic plan, they could then accomplish more and, in turn, become more excited about their lives. Thus was born the idea for this book.

Dr. Linneman grew up in the small Midwestern town of Bloomington, Illinois. He received a bachelor's degree from Illinois Wesleyan University in 1950. Shortly thereafter he enlisted in the United States Air Force. He served three months as an enlisted man and then entered an air cadet training program—navigation school. Upon graduation he was commissioned a second lieutenant and served until 1955 as a navigator–bombardier–radar operator on a B-36 in the Strategic Air Command. In the succeeding five years he gained business experience through farming, farm management, and industrial sales.

In 1960 he entered graduate school at the University of Illinois,

where in 1962 he received an M.S. in Marketing and in 1964 a
Ph.D., also in Marketing. In 1964 he joined the faculty of Temple University as Assistant Professor of Marketing.

In addition to his consulting and teaching activities, Dr. Linneman has participated in the design, marketing, and presentation
of executive development programs throughout the United States,
and is an enthusiastic speaker at sales and marketing conven-
tions. He has written articles for several professional journals.

Professor Linneman is married, has two children, and resides
in Valley Forge, Pennsylvania.

# Preface

This book is specifically designed for the student who is not quite certain what he wants out of life.

Actually, few people know how to point their lives toward success; the majority consequently go through life only partly "turned on." A major weakness in today's educational system is that it fails to provide students with practical guidance for life planning. Some lucky few are able to work out their own goals, but life planning is too important a procedure to be left to chance. A person should have practical guidance.

The fact is, most students need professional advice. The purpose of this book is *not* to take the place of the professional guidance counselor. Indeed, such an expert provides a flexibility in counseling that is impossible to match on the printed page. Rather, the book is designed to act as a supplement.

As a marketing professor, it has frequently been my privilege to advise students in their vocational choices. But sometimes I have been of little help: They were unable to articulate what they wanted out of life. Without this information, job counseling becomes little more than pulling a name out of a hat. How could I have suggested a "road" for them to follow when they were uncertain where they wanted to go? This same situation often handicaps professional counselors in their work.

This book is designed to assist a student by providing a highly structured step-by-step procedure for him to follow in establishing his goals in life. It does not suggest what a person's goals should be; rather it helps the goal setter articulate what it is that he wants out of life. He will then be in a better position to plan his life.

If the student then wishes to seek the advice of a professional counselor, he will have certain advantages. He will be able to tell the vocational guidance counselor, for instance, specific things he would like to gain from his life's work. Knowing this, the vocational guidance counselor will then be in a better position to tell the student what kinds of jobs he should consider.

Although the terminology in this book is geared for high-school and university male students, female students and, indeed, persons of all ages and in all walks of life will find it helpful in structuring their life for the future.

I would like to express my thanks to many individuals who have helped to make this book possible. Above all, special appreciation should be given to Professor Paul Dauten, who taught me the meaning of a goal; to Professors Harvey Huegy and Lloyd DeBoer, who so unselfishly spent hours of their time trying to teach me to think logically and to put my thoughts on paper; to Professor Dwight Flanders, who introduced me to a "wonderful world of models"; and to Dr. Philip Harris, who gave me a bit of advice: "Spend your life doing things you really want to do." I also wish to thank Miss Nancy Schiff, who was very helpful in typing this manuscript in its early stages of development, and Miss Hope Stringer, who spent hours on later drafts.

Robert E. Linneman, Ph.D.

# Contents

## CHAPTER I

## *Introduction*
## *(Time Required: 10 minutes)*

Turn yourself on?
Why not?
This is how others have become excited about their lives.[1]

*Case History Number 1*

October was almost over. Paul was in his last year of high school, and he felt more uneasy with every passing day. Most of the other seniors had already sent in their college applications, but Paul could not get himself to sit down and decide where to apply.

Somehow this indecision made him feel unmanly and even babyish, but for the life of him he just couldn't figure out what he wanted to do when he got out of college. He almost wished he could go back a year or two. College would mean a sacrifice for his parents, and Paul was beginning to think that maybe it would be better to forget it. "Unless you can figure out what you want to do with your life, how can you decide on the right college to prepare you for it?" Then, too, there was the uncertainty about his service obligation.

It was not that Paul had never thought about what he wanted to do. He had talked with vocational guidance counselors, friends, and teachers. Most of them had made suggestions, but after investigation none of the suggested plans seemed right for him.

---

[1] I first started working on this book in 1962. During this period I discussed the concepts and methodology with many friends, students, guidance counselors, and fellow teachers. Manuscripts were given to a number of people. These case histories typify results that were accomplished.

Paul was frustrated. Here he was, about to be graduated—with good grades—and yet he had no idea what he should do next. It was ironical: This should be a supreme moment, a moment of glory, a moment of "Look out, world, here I come!" But it was not. Paul felt despondent and insecure.

One of his friends, Bill, was faced with a similar problem. But Bill had gone to a vocational guidance counselor, who, when he found out that Bill couldn't express what it was he wanted out of life, suggested that Bill read *Turn Yourself On*. After Bill read the book, he recommended it to Paul.

Paul read the book, and by following the step-by-step procedures contained in it, he was able to establish explicit goals. For the first time in his life he was able to state what it was he really wanted out of life. In his continuing search for a life's occupation, he found that these goals acted as a good screening device: He could quickly discard occupations that would not allow him to meet his Must Goals. He also found that once he told others— vocational guidance counselors, friends, teachers—what it was he wanted out of life, they were able to give him more meaningful advice. Not only that, Paul began to feel like a man who could make decisions.

After some search, Paul decided to point himself toward a career in advertising. Selecting colleges made sense for the first time: He now knew specifically what it was he wanted out of a college education.

Today Paul is working toward a degree in a Midwestern university that has an excellent advertising department. Paul is enthusiastic about his studies because they relate to the plans he has made for his life.

*Case History Number 2*

Harold had wished that the last few months of high school would pass quickly: There had been too many awkward moments. He had been in groups where classmates talked enthusiastically of their college plans, and then, remembering that Harold was not going on, told him how lucky he was to be finishing school. Sometimes they had not been so kind. And numerous other thorny occasions had arisen. For example, one night when he was calling for his date, her mother had asked him, "What college are you going to, Harold?" He would not soon forget how he had fumbled for an answer and how his face had flushed.

He had sensed his parents' disappointment. True, they had told him that anything he wanted to do was all right with them, but their subtle implications had indicated that this was not so. Secretly, though he would not admit it to others, Harold was disappointed in himself. How could he get excited about his life? How could he hope to succeed? Others had always been so much quicker than he in school.

In fact, he had never been successful in school. He had always had trouble in mathematics and English. He had decided he would not even apply for college admission: What would be the use? Why spend another four years in torment and, no doubt, end in failure? But then, without a college education he would have to settle for a "second-rate" career.

Harold did not have much time to think about careers after high school, since he was soon drafted. Upon completion of basic training, he was sent to a motor vehicle depot. He did not particularly like it, but at least for the moment he had no worries about job hunting.

The months passed uneventfully and steadily, and once again Harold was faced with "the question." He would be discharged before long and would have to decide upon a career. But he was no further along with developing plans than he had been in high school.

One night at a USO center, Harold happened to see a copy of *Turn Yourself On*. Intrigued, he started reading it. He soon realized that he had been making a common mistake—he had been confusing means with ends. A college education was just a means to an end, not an end itself. He could achieve what he really wanted out of life in many ways besides going to college. Using the book as a guide, he set specific stimulating goals. He then sought help at the guidance center at his Army post. It was decided that he could best meet his goals if he became a real-estate broker.

Today, Harold is happily employed as a real-estate salesman. He is doing quite well and hopes eventually to open his own office. He is no longer disturbed by his poor performance in school, since he now knows that he can achieve his goals in many ways other than by going to college. He is now successfully "turned on."

*Case History Number 3*

John's problem was one that had been created by his parents. Since the day John was born they had talked about the time when he would become a doctor. Although they were in the lower-middle-class income bracket—hardly in a position to afford the costly years of education—they had started making sacrifices early in John's life. Now they were able to send him to college and medical school.

But John had no interest in science. In high school his work was only average in science subjects, but good to excellent in all his other courses. In response to his parents' plans, he enrolled in a pre-med course when he entered college. Although his marks were satisfactory, he was not enthusiastic about his school work, nor, for that matter, his life in general. He would have liked to change his curriculum, but he knew how such a switch would upset his parents.

By chance he came across a copy of *Turn Yourself On*. While reading Chapter II he realized a basic error his parents had been making: They had been thinking of a career (medicine) as an end rather than a means to an end. For example, why had they always wanted him to become a doctor? Was it because they wanted him:

> to go through long years of schooling?
> to wear a white coat?
> to get his hands bloody?
> to make house calls in the middle of the night?

These, of course, were not the reasons at all. They had wanted him to have, among other things, a certain level of income, a certain degree of respect from his fellow men, and to make a contribution to society. They had insisted that John be a doctor because they felt this was the best way he could achieve these goals. They failed to realize the many other occupations that would enable him to reach the same desired ends. They failed to see that John's aptitudes and interests might be better served if he planned to reach these desired ends through some other sort of occupation.

John discussed the situation with his parents. He outlined his objectives and was relieved to see their disappointment turn to admiration when they realized that although John insisted upon choosing the means, the end was the one they had always wished for him.

John went to the vocational guidance center at his university. After a careful review of his objectives and testing of his interests and abilities, it was recommended that he think in terms of city planning as a life's work. John followed this advice. Today he is in graduate school pursuing a career of city planning, and is very much excited about his life and his work.

*    *    *

In each of the situations discussed above, vocational adjustment was greatly aided by the use of this book. But of even greater importance, each of these individuals learned to manage his own life. A career is certainly a significant part of life, but it is *only a part*. These men learned to establish clearly defined, exciting life objectives before seeking a career. They had all probably been advised to set goals at one time or another. What they needed was advice on how to do it. When they found out how to set meaningful goals, Paul, Harold, and John also discovered that:

- they had a better basis for action.
- they became more decisive.
- they developed a better sense of purpose.

- they became more enthusiastic.
- they were able to utilize their time in a more profitable manner.

Instead of *hoping* for the best, they decided to *plan* for the best.

Unfortunately, too many people believe that somehow, somewhere, they will be "turned on." Without plans or goals, they follow others. But other people are seldom interested in planning the lives of their followers. Often enough, they are not even able to plan their own lives, in which case the follower ends up in a predicament experienced by the processionary caterpillars in an experiment once conducted by the French naturalist Jean Henri Fabre. Processionary caterpillars are so named because in their search for food, they follow one another with eyes nearly closed and head pressed to the rear extremity of the one ahead. Fabre arranged a group of these caterpillars on the rim of a flowerpot, in a circle, one connected to the next. Although food and water were in plain sight, they kept up their relentless circular pace, one following the other. Only complete exhaustion and near starvation succeeded in halting their meaningless pursuit of absolute nothing!

## Can This Book Help You?

Although no one can promise you success, *your chances for success are far better if you are working toward specific objectives.* If you follow this method of life managing, you too will achieve the benefits listed above. You will become more excited; your odds for success will be improved.

This book gives simple steps for you to follow in establishing your personal goals. The principles embodied in these steps are not abstract theories that have little application. On the contrary, they are being used today by many successful business firms in their planning operations. The unique aspect of this book is the application of these principles to the planning processes for management of one's personal life.

In this book you will program all aspects of your life: occupational, financial, and personal. I am sure you are aware of men who have become highly successful in business and yet whose lives are actually failures: In their drive for success in business, they have neglected their families and, as a consequence, ruined their family lives. Here, however, such shortsightedness is avoided, since you will be programming all aspects of your life.

The approach taken in this book is not a moralistic one. It does not attempt to tell you what you should strive for. Rather, this book is designed to explain to you what to do to achieve success—regardless of what success means to you.

*Organization of the Book*

Let us explain how the book is organized. Basic rules to follow in setting goals are given in Chapter II. In Chapter III and IV you will actually set your personal goals. The procedure is highly structured. Alternatives are given, so in most cases all you need do is choose among those stated. Chapter V contains a format to follow in developing plans to carry out your life goals. Also included in this chapter are tips on where to find information about scholarships, the draft, vocations, and personal guidance.

After you finish the book, you will have clearly defined goals—bases for action—probably for the first time in your life. Then you will begin to enjoy the power of those who manage by objectives.

*A word of caution:* Do not make the mistake of working through Chapters III and IV without *first* reading Chapter II. It is very important that Chapter II be read first, because it provides the conceptual framework.

*How Much Work Will Be Involved?*

You will be able to read the book and establish your life objectives in less than five hours!

So that you can better schedule your activities, the average time required for completion is stated at the beginning of each chapter.

Do not attempt to finish the book in one sitting. It is best to allow time intervals between certain activities so that you will have "fresh" approaches. Consequently, the following schedule is recommended:

|              |                        | Average Time Required |
|--------------|------------------------|-----------------------|
| First Day:   | Chapters I and II      | 25 min.               |
| Second Day:  | Chapter III            | 1 1/2 hrs.            |
| Third Day:   | Review of Chapter III  | 15 min.               |
| Fourth Day:  | Chapter IV             | 1 1/2 hrs.            |
| Fifth Day:   | Review of Chapter IV   | 15 min.               |
| Sixth Day:   | Chapter V              | 30 min.               |

## CHAPTER II

## *Rules to Follow in Establishing Goals (Time Required: 15 minutes)*

Successful business firms follow certain prescribed rules or principles in establishing goals. These principles provide broad guidelines for the planners and help them to avoid pointless or impossible goals. They have been adapted in this chapter for use in personal goal setting.

Do not concern yourself about setting your goals while reading this chapter. In Chapters III and IV, you will be shown how to establish your own personal goals, step by step.

### *Goals Should Be Set for Things You Really Want to Achieve*

Many people tend to be occupation (means)-oriented instead of being goal-oriented. For example, ask a classmate what he really wants out of life. He'll probaby say, "To be a doctor," "To be a lawyer," or name some other occupation. But does this person really want to be a doctor, or does he want certain things —such as money, prestige, social position, the feeling of service to mankind—which he feels he will attain by being a doctor? It is a *type of life* the person is really seeking, and the occupation (being a doctor) is only a means, a strategy, for achieving this type of life.

Unfortunately, by being means-oriented one reduces the possibility of living a well-satisfied life. Let us carry the above example one step further. When a person states "I want to be a doctor," he has eliminated dozens of other means of attaining the type of life he is seeking. Until he has established goals and taken an inventory of himself and the opportunities available to him, he should avoid reducing his alternatives. The person may

19

lack—and be unable to acquire—the aptitude to complete medical school successfully. Furthermore, attempts to gain this required aptitude may be frustrating and disillusioning.

A person can follow many occupations in order to achieve a certain amount of money, prestige, social status, and service to mankind. To be sure, after establishing objectives, performing a self-analysis, and examining the opportunities available, the person may decide that he can attain his goals with less effort by becoming a doctor than by any other means. Fine! But note: One should not decide upon the means until one has established what it is he really wants out of life, taken an inventory of himself, and examined the opportunities available to him. This procedure greatly enhances the possibility of living a well-satisfied life.

Incidentally, much of the doubt concerning human capabilities stems from confusing jobs with objectives in life. Nearly everyone has the capability of being great—but only a few have the capability of becoming, for example, a great pro basketball player.

### Goals Should Be Specific

Most people do not have specific goals. Ask a person if he has goals. If he says, "Yes," then ask him, "What are your goals?" Usually, the answer will include some of the "goals" mentioned below:

- to have a good life.
- to be successful.
- to have a happy marriage.
- to aid my fellow man.
- to educate my children.
- to be able to retire early.
- to devote more time to my favorite hobby.
- to make this a better world.

But suppose you then say, for instance, "Well, it's fine that you want to have a good life. But what do you mean by a 'good life?' " Invariably, the individual will be unable to explain—in specific terms—what he means by a "good life."

Goals are supposed to provide blueprints for action. But how can such a goal as "the good life" provide a blueprint for action if one cannot define what he means by "the good life"? How can this general goal tell him where he should concentrate his energies?

In fact, all eight "goals" listed above are nothing more than sweeping generalizations. They are too vague to give any definite suggestions as to what one should be doing in his everyday life. A management authority, Manley Howe Jones, points out that ". . . sweeping generalizations about man's needs and aspirations are not much use in determining the goals of an individual. . . "[1]

Several rules should be remembered in establishing specific goals.

First, a goal should be measurable. It should be an intended outcome, and/or describe what you will be doing when you reach your goal. Following this rule, then, a "goal" of being "financially successful" is not actually a goal. It is not a measurable intended outcome, nor does it tell one what he will be doing when he is financially successful. One cannot tell when he has reached his goal. Such a "goal" is meaningless.

This goal can be restated so that it becomes meaningful. Say, "Financial success will be met if I am making $20,000 a year by the time I am 40 years old, and if I have saved $20,000 (in life insurance, stocks and bonds, savings accounts, or some other form of measurable savings)." This is a meaningful goal because you know what you will be doing (or what you will have) when you reach the goal.

It is critical that you attach a definite time period for the accomplishment of your goals. Let us look at the hypothetical financial goal just mentioned:

---

[1] Manley Howe Jones, *Executive Decision Making,* Rev. ed., Homewood, Ill.: Richard D. Irwin, Inc., 1962, p. 115.

". . . making $20,000 a year by the time I am 40 years old and . . . have saved $20,000 . . ." Notice that this goal is to be reached within a definite time period.

The above example also highlights another very important principle: If possible, you should state your goals in terms of quality, dollars, percentages, or proportions.

Financial goals are the easiest to quantify. They are the easiest to state in specific terms. However, it is recognized that most people want more out of life than financial rewards. They may want, for example, to be happily married. How does one quantify this? In such cases in which you cannot set up numerical standards, you should specify (write out) what the optimum conditions should be. In Chapter III you will find a practical system that will help you state in specific terms goals that are difficult to quantify.

To summarize this section, the following are criteria that you can use to test the specificity of your goals:

Are they measurable? Will you know when you have reached these goals?

Are they quantified? Are they expressed in terms of quality, dollars, percentages, or proportions?

If goals cannot be quantified, have you specified what the optimum conditions should be?

Have you established a definite time period for achievement of your goals?

If you can answer these questions in the affirmative, your goals are specific.

*Goals Should Be Set for Every Area in Which Performance and Results Significantly Affect Your Happiness*

How simple it would be to manage our lives if we had only one specific thing we wanted out of life! However, an individual usually has a *set* of *many* goals that he is trying to achieve. And, unless he has well-defined goals for each significant area that affects his happiness, he may find his actions "out-of-balance." The result will be unhappiness.

Let me give an example. Suppose a person has the desire to be a success in his job, to have a happy married life, and to raise fine children. The individual views being successful in his job as "being district sales manager of the firm by the time I'm 30." He does not, however, set clearly defined objectives for his other goals. Consequently, he tends to concentrate his energies on being successful in his job. For this goal he has targets to meet; he knows what he is expected to do if he is to attain his objective of being district sales manager. He lacks such measurable criteria in his marital and family life, however, and as a result neglects these areas.

Eventually he becomes district sales manager. But he finds himself very unhappy. He had visions of having a happy married life, but he now finds himself divorced. He had wanted a close relationship with his children, but his wife has custody of the children.

What had gone wrong? He had failed to establish specific goals for his family life. As a result, he had neglected working toward the achievement of a happy family life, and this type of life did not "just happen."

Most individuals are concerned with other things besides money or success in their jobs. Consequently, *goals are needed in every area in which performance and results significantly affect the happiness of the person,* not just for a person's financial or vocational success.

A common mistake is trying to cover too many goals under one heading. "To have a good life" is a good illustration of this fault. If you define what you mean by having a good life, then you will be likely to come up with three or four goals instead of the one. The more goals you list, the clearer you can see what you are trying to achieve in life. Furthermore, you are following a management principle by dividing a complicated, vague problem into its component parts—thus enabling you to identify and solve the less complicated segments.

You should recognize, however, as a practical matter you cannot set goals for each and every facet of your life. Raymond

F. Valentine suggests that "key objectives"—covering the most important desires—be established. By so doing, one will "eliminate the sense of vagueness and unreality associated with lengthy lists of goals . . ." [1] When you set your goals in Chapter III and IV, you will be limiting your objective to the major desires of your life, to "key-objective" areas.

### Goals Should Be Ranked in Order of Preference

The preceding section has pointed out how an individual has a set of many desires in life. To further complicate matters, occasionally some of these desires may be in conflict with one another—to fulfill one you have to give up another.

An examination of a person's goals usually reveals that some are more important than others. [2] Thus, if you are to manage your life efficiently and effectively, you must develop a clear picture of the relative importance of the goals you wish to attain, so that you can give priority to those goals you feel are the most important. You should follow a plan for utilizing your time, such as the French concept of *triage* (selection). Let's look at *triage* in action.

*Triage* is a method for allocating scarce resources. For example, suppose a division of the army has limited medical facilities, being able to accommodate only 100 injured soldiers. However, in a battle 300 are wounded. If all the wounded are given attention, the facilities would be spread so thin that the care given to each patient would be almost worthless.

*Triage* offers a system for maximizing the use of the facilities. The first step is to categorize the wounded into three classes. The first class would be the "walking wounded." These men would

---

[1] Raymond F. Valentine, *Performance Objectives for Managers,* Brattleboro, Vt.: The Book Press, 1966, p. 56.

[2] To be sure, the importance attached to various goals may vary from person to person. To one person, money may be most important. He may not care what kind of job he has to do, so long as the money is there. To another person, pay may be a secondary consideration if the job has prestige. Each person has a different set of values, and accordingly, attaches different degrees of importance to different goals.

actually be able to treat themselves. Although they might be suffering considerable pain, they could get by without care. The second group would consist of men requiring more extensive treatment and more time for healing. The third group would be those who were almost mortally wounded.

Following the concept of *triage*, the medical field station would treat the wounded in the following manner: No treatment would be given to the walking wounded; all facilities would be devoted to the second class of wounded. If after treating this group there still remained time, supplies, and facilities, then the third class would be cared for. If, however, there were only enough medical personnel, supplies, and facilities to care for the second class, the third group would be left to die unattended.

At first this sounds very cold-blooded—indeed, heartless. But is there a fairer way? In this way the maximum number of lives is saved.

An interesting method has been devised for ranking goals.[1] You cannot possibly set goals for everything in life. As a practical matter, therefore, you should select the things most important to you and concentrate your efforts on these goals.

An interesting method has been devised for ranking goals.[2] This technique, developed for business managers, has been modified to make it suitable for establishing personal goals, and is presented here. Three basic categories of goals are established:

1. Must Goals: These are so important that we consider them absolutely essential.
2. Want Goals: These are important, but we do not consider them absolutely essential to success.
3. Unimportant Goals: These goals might be nice to have, but it does not matter much one way or the other if they are obtained.

Category 1 (Must Goals) and Category 2 (Want Goals)

[1] Charles H. Kepner and Benjamin B. Tregoe, *The Rational Manager,* New York: McGraw-Hill Book Company, 1965.

consist of goals that would be used as the framework for determining "key objectives." Category 3, on the other hand (Unimportant Goals), contains goals not considered worthy of inclusion in a list of goals.

Must Goals, then, are goals to be attained at all costs. There is no hierarchy among these goals. They all must be attained. Must Goals are of a higher order than Want Goals. Want Goals are those that would be nice to have but are not absolutely essential. There is a hierarchy among these goals.

Perhaps an example would help to clarify these concepts. A person feels that he must have a minimum annual income of $15,000 twenty years from now. The $15,000 salary is a Must Goal. On the other hand, he would *like* to have an income of $40,000, but does *not* consider it absolutely essential. This extra $25,000 a year is a Want Goal. This individual also considers it *absolutely essential* that he live in a $30,000 home twenty years from now. This is a Must Goal. He would *like* to be living in a $70,000 home, but he does *not* feel it absolutely mandatory. The extra $40,000 (which would bring the $30,000 house up to $70,000) is a Want Goal.

This individual, then, has established two Must Goals that he feels must be attained at all costs:

1. A minimum annual income of $15,000.
2. A $30,000 home.

These Must Goals act as a quick screening tool to indicate what courses of action should be followed. Any courses of action that are not likely to allow for the accomplishment of these two goals should be promptly discarded.

If a person has several courses of action he can follow to meet his Must Goals, then he uses Want Goals to help him decide which of these plans he should follow. For example, if several alternative courses of action are available to you (that will enable you to meet your Must Goals) and you are trying to decide which one you should implement, I suggest you use the following procedure.

1. Carefully study each course of action. What are the extras —over and above the "musts"—that each plan is likely to provide? Make a list of extras for each course of action.
2. Examine these lists; then rank the items in order of preference.

Following this procedure, you will be able to determine which plan of action will provide you with the most extras.

The value of this system can be seen clearly. It provides a blueprint for evaluating courses of action. One can discard immediately those that do not enable him to reach his Must Goals. After this initial screening, one can evaluate the remaining plans in relation to the Want Goals that they can achieve. He then selects the course of action that offers the most Want Goals. Such a system enables a person to become more decisive and to concentrate his energies.

*Goals Should Be Visionary, Yet Believable*

Executives realize the necessity for visionary corporate goals. Frederick R. Kappel, former chairman of the American Telephone and Telegraph Company, states that unless a business sets demanding and exciting goals, it runs the risk of losing vitality.[1]

This principle holds true for setting personal goals. Unless your efforts are directed toward something you *really* want, why should you put forth any effort? The amount of energy you are willing to expend varies almost directly with the intensity of your desire. Little desire almost always means low-level achievement. On the other hand, if you are working toward goals you really want to attain, you are willing to work and you develop persist-

---

[1] *Vitality in a Business Enterprise,* New York: McGraw-Hill Book Company, 1960, pp. 37–38.

ence. You gain the "vitality" that Frederick Kappel recognized as being so important. Visionary goals, then, release powers, yes —the genius within you. No wonder Napoleon said, "Imagination rules the world!"

Yet it does little good to establish goals at a level you do not believe you can actually reach. If you do not believe you can accomplish your goals, you will not develop plans to achieve them. Furthermore, negative thoughts will prevent you from developing enthusiasm and persistence, thus robbing you of powers necessary for high-level performance.

You *must* believe that you have the ability to achieve what you really want out of life. Do you have serious doubts about your ability for such achievement? If your answer is "yes," STOP. Turn to Chapter VI, *Shoot for the Moon.*

Where should you set your goals? Perhaps it is best summed up once again by Kappel, who states: "Part of the talent or genius of the goal setter is the ability to distinguish between the possible and impossible—but to be willing to get very close to the latter." [1]

*Goals Should Be Tailor-made*

What do you want out of life? What will give you satisfaction? This must be decided by you and you alone. Your goals, then, must be tailor-made.

There are several reasons for this. In the first place, few people have the same background and want identical things out of life. Happiness means different things to different people: To Albert Schweitzer it meant serving mankind; to Alexander and Julius Caesar it was power; to Billy Graham it is serving God. The famed psychiatrist Carl Rogers notes that the most effective personal adjustments come about only after individuals establish meaningful personal goals. What are "meaningful personal goals"? Things that they as individuals really want to attain.[2]

---

[1] Charles H. Granger, "The Hierarchy of Objectives," *Harvard Business Review,* May–June, 1964.

[2] Carl Rogers, *A Therapist's View of Personal Goals,* Wallingford, Pa.: Pendle Hill, 1960.

A management scholar, George R. Terry, offers another good reason that goals should be self-made: ". . . there is a tendency for people to set higher goals for themselves than others would set for them." [1] Higher goals, of course, stimulate greater achievement.

The third reason that your goals should be tailor-made is to escape, as much as possible, negative environmental influences. If you let others set your goals for you, the goals will probably be those of your environment. This could act as a detriment to you.

## Goals Should Be Committed to Writing

A very good reason for one to go through the actual process of writing out his goals is that doing so demands more rigorous thinking.

For example, did you ever have a strong mental image of something, but, in trying to communicate the idea to someone else, find that you could not effectively express your ideas? This was probably because the image you had was pretty "fuzzy," and you had allowed yourself to gloss over many critical points. When you tried to convey your idea to others, you began to realize that the idea needed further thought. We are subject to this same kind of "fuzzy" thinking in setting goals. This danger can be eliminated, however, by committing the goals to writing.

## Goals Should Not Be Considered Irrevocable

Some people object to establishing goals and making long-range plans. They argue, "I don't know what the future is going to be like. I really can't set goals and make long-range plans. I'll have to wait and see. In ten years I may want something entirely different from what I have now. So how can I set long-range goals?"

It is agreed that in ten years you may have an entirely different

---

[1] George R. Terry, *Principles of Management,* Homewood, Ill.: Richard D. Irwin, Inc., 1964, p. 39.

outlook on life. As you move through time and your environment, you will change. As you change, so will your goals. Therefore, in establishing your goals, you must consider them as aims that may be expanded, contracted, or eliminated. Your goals should not be considered irrevocable. As a matter of fact, you should make provision for periodic review of your goals. During these examinations you should ask: "Has anything happened that would make me want to change my goals?" If the answer is in the affirmative, the goals should be changed.

However, this does not negate the need for you to establish goals now. Unless you have specific goals, you will become the victim of indecision and mismanaged effort. Without objectives, your chances for a happy life are greatly reduced.

### SUMMARY

This chapter has presented eight rules to be followed in establishing goals.

- Goals should be set for things you really want to achieve.
- Goals should be specific.
- Goals should be set for every area in which performance and results significantly affect your happiness.
- Goals should be ranked in order of preference.
- Goals should be visionary, yet believable.
- Goals should be tailor-made.
- Goals should be committed to writing.
- Goals should not be considered irrevocable.

These eight principles should be kept in mind while developing goals.

I advise you to stop for now. The next chapter will take about one and one-half hours. If possible, read it tomorrow—preferably early in the day when your mind is fresh.

## CHAPTER III

# A Programmed Procedure for Goal Setting (Time Required: 1½ hours)

This is what you will accomplish in this chapter:

First, you will determine your planning horizon and interim target dates.
Next, you will establish Must Goals for your planning horizon and interim target dates.

*        *        *

*Determination of Your Planning Horizon*
*and Interim Target Dates*

You should plan to accomplish your goals within a specific number of years. This time span is called the "planning horizon"; the goals established for the end of this period are called "planning horizon goals."

Use caution in establishing the length of your planning horizon. A very short planning horizon will probably not allow you enough time to develop the traits necessary for your goal accomplishment.

For example, students often say, "This semester I'm going to do 'A' work." They do work hard, and yet many wind up at the end of the semester with a "C" average. Why? In most cases they lack the necessary skills to do "A" work. They do not know how to study, how to read rapidly with comprehension, or how to express themselves effectively.

Hard work cannot compensate for basic deficiencies if your planning horizon is too short. It is almost like racing an untrained horse and then whipping the horse because it cannot run the mile and a quarter in 2:02.

31

On the other hand, goals for the too-distant future also have their drawbacks. For most people, a planning horizon of thirty or forty years has the disadvantage of being too remote to seem attainable.

Therefore, you should set your planning horizon far enough in the future to make accomplishment realistic, yet close enough so that you can visualize yourself benefiting from your efforts.

Although it is essential for an individual to establish a planning horizon and Must Goals for this date, it is also necessary to set goals for specific target dates during the planning horizon. These goals are called "interim goals," and the time periods are called "interim target dates."

An example will illustrate the necessity of establishing interim goals. A person may establish a Must Goal of a $20,000 annual salary for the end of his ten-year planning horizon. Yet he does not want to live like a recluse for the next ten years to attain this goal. He feels that he MUST earn at least $7,000 annually for the first five years and $10,000 a year for the next five: indeed, these "interim musts" are as important to this person as is his $20,000 planning horizon Must Goal. You may have similar "interim musts." You will find that it facilitates planning if you have them clearly in mind.

There are other reasons for establishing interim Must Goals. When you set your planning horizon Must Goals, the relationships with your family and friends are geared toward the end of your planning horizon. When setting these goals, you take into account such uncontrollable factors as the death of aging relatives and the inevitable changes in your physical and emotional needs. If your parents are over 70 years old, you probably do not consider them a part of your planning horizon Must Goals. Also, if you are married or contemplating marriage, at certain stages of your marriage your spouse may require more of your time and assistance than at others.

*A word of caution: You are not—repeat not—making plans when you are determining your interim Must Goals. You are in*

fact clarifying and defining what you feel your life must be between now and the end of your planning horizon. Consequently,
when establishing interim Must Goals, do not think of them as
means to attain planning horizon Must Goals—think of them as
things you feel you *must* have.

Although the "best" time spans for planning horizons and interim target dates vary—depending upon the particular needs of
the individual—for the vast majority of students the following are
recommended:

- Planning horizon (terminal date)—ten years from now.
- First interim target date—one year from now.
- Second interim target date—five years from now.

Determine what planning horizon and interim target dates seem
suitable for you and then record them in the appropriate columns
on pages 51 through 67.

If you are using a library book, then I would suggest:

- Have copies made of pages 51 through 67. Most libraries
  have copying machines available for your use.
- If, however, you cannot use a copying machine, then construct forms similar to the one on the next page.

*Determination of Your Planning Horizon*
*and Interim Target Date Must Goals*

*Note: You are considering only goals you consider absolutely*
*essential.* For now, do not worry about goals you would *like* to
attain. These goals are Want Goals, and in a later chapter you
will take them into account. You will recall our discussion of the
hierarchy of goals and why Must Goals and Want Goals should
be determined separately. If these concepts seem fuzzy to you, I
strongly urge you to reread pages 24 to 28.

A number of goals are listed on pages 51 to 58. This section
is structured so that all you need do, in most cases, is check the
appropriate box. (If you are using the substitute form suggested
above, then write your Must Goals in the Must Goal column and
the description in the appropriate date columns. Merely ignore

| Must Goals | First Interim Target Date ___ | Second Interim Target Date ___ | Planning Horizon Target Date ___ |
|---|---|---|---|
|  |  |  |  |
|  |  |  |  |
|  |  |  |  |
|  |  |  |  |
|  |  |  |  |
|  |  |  |  |
|  |  |  |  |
|  |  |  |  |
|  |  |  |  |
|  |  |  |  |

the suggested goals that are "not too important" to you.) While establishing your goals it is *essential* that you read the Guide for Establishing Goals and then complete the corresponding section in the Must Goal list.

For example, the first section in the Guide for Establishing Goals (page 36) explains how to establish your minimum annual salary "musts." After you have read this section, fill in the Minimum Annual Salary column on page 51. And so on.

Below are some general rules to follow in establishing your Must Goals.

- View each goal as being *completely separate* from others.
- *Do not* try to mold goals to conform to an occupation.
- For now, *do not* concern yourself with how you will attain these goals. (In Chapter V you will be shown how you can determine the means—for instance, occupations—you can use to reach these goals.)
- Consider only those goals that you think are *absolutely essential* for you to reach by the end of your planning horizon and for the interim target dates.
- Do not try to be "conventional" and write in what you think is expected of you. No one is going to see your lists except yourself.
- For those goals that require dollar sums, use current dollar values.
- It is usually advisable to set your planning horizon Must Goals first, then set your interim target date Must Goals.
- *Set your goals for things you really want to achieve.*

REMEMBER: *YOU ARE CONSIDERING ONLY GOALS THAT YOU BELIEVE TO BE ABSOLUTELY ESSENTIAL.*

*    *    *

Do not worry if you find yourself checking a considerable number of the "Not Too Important" boxes. So much the better. By this process of elimination, you will be isolating the things that are extremely important to you. A short list of goals makes it easier to concentrate on these "musts."

## Guide for Establishing Goals

### Occupational Goals

*Minimum Annual Salary*—Do you feel you must have a certain minimum annual salary by the end of your planning horizon and/or interim target dates? If not, check the "Not Important" box.

If you feel it is absolutely essential that you have a minimum annual salary, what is the least sum you would consider absolutely necessary to feel successful at the end of your planning horizon? At the end of your interim target dates? Write these figures in the space provided.

*Type of Employment*—How do you feel about being self-employed as opposed to working for an employer? If you feel it would be absolutely essential for your success to be working for someone else, check this box.

If you feel it would be absolutely essential to be self-employed, check this box.

If it does not matter, check "Not Too Important." Do this for all three dates.

*Size of Firm*—Some individuals feel it a "must" in life to be associated with a large firm. They believe such an affiliation will give them prestige.

Others take the opposite view: they feel it mandatory to work for a small firm, in which they can experience a more intimate relationship.

36

Still others feel it a "must" to work for a medium-size firm, in which they can experience the "best of both worlds."

Finally, some individuals are not concerned about the size of the firm—if everything else is right.

Check your "must." (Assume the following definitions: small firm, 1–199 employees; medium-size firm, 200–1,000 employees; large firm, above 1,000.)

*Geographic Area Preference*—Is there some geographic area in which you feel you *must* be working at the end of your planning horizon? During the interim? For example, several individuals have told me they would never move from the Philadelphia Main Line. Perhaps you feel that way about some area. If so, in the space provided, specify the location in which you feel you *must* work.

*Type of Work* (Technical Skills, Managerial Skills)—Some people feel it most essential that they have a job in which they can develop their technical skill without spending a considerable amount of time managing people. Illustrative of such jobs of a technical nature are those of research chemists, artists, writers, doctors, and highly skilled machinists.

On the other hand, it is a must for some people to have a job that involves managing others. They are not interested in developing technical skills. They would rather be able to get things done through people.

To others it doesn't really matter whether the job be technical or managerial.

Check your musts for each of the dates.

*Travel* (Away from Home)—Some people are not happy unless they have a job demanding a great deal of travel.

Others are discontented if they must be away from home for even short periods of time.

What is your "must" preference? If travel is not important to

you, check the "Not Too Important" box. If, however, you feel
you must be home every night, do not check that box. Or, if you
feel you must spend some time away from home, check the box
best representing your "musts."

*Speeches and Public Appearances*—I think we all know people
who are petrified to give a speech in public and furthermore have
no desire to correct this fear. To this kind of person, a "must"
would be to have a job requiring very few or no public appearances.

We also know people who are just the opposite. Their "must"
would be to have a job placing them in the limelight as much as
possible.

What is your "must" considering the following definitions:

> Very few: no more than one formal speech per month.
> Some: no more than three formal speeches per month.
> Frequent: at least one formal speech per week.

*Job Security*—Do you consider it absolutely essential that you
have a job with a company that gives you a feeling of security? Is
it a must that you have such a relationship with the company that
you need not worry about being fired or laid off? (A civil-service
appointment is an example of this type of security.) If so, check
"Very Stable."

If, however, you do not feel it a "must" that you have the above
type of security—and yet you would like to avoid the volatility
found in advertising agencies, for example, then check "Moder-
ately Stable."

If job security is not really important to you, check that box.

*Job Flexibility*—Is it a "must" that you have a job enabling
you to take a vacation almost whenever you please? A job in
which you could take off in the middle of the week—almost on
the spur of the moment—for perhaps a two-day golfing or fishing
trip? If so, check "Extremely Flexible Schedule."

Or perhaps you feel you "must" have a fixed schedule, possibly a job with regular 9-to-5 hours in which you could count on having your weekends free and vacations at a certain time every year.

Or perhaps you are indifferent to the type of schedule you would have as long as other job factors are satisfactory.

Check the appropriate square.

*Working Environment* (Physical)—How important are physical facilities to you? To some persons, a good physical plant—including such amenities as carpeting, air conditioning, parking—is a "must." Others would not want a job requiring them to spend their working hours indoors. They want to work outside.

On the other hand, many persons do not really care about these things. As long as the money is right—or the challenge of the job is right—the physical environment means little to them.

Which of these categories best describes your "must" desires?

*Working Environment* (Companion Relationships)—Certain people view favorable working companion relationships as a "must" condition. Since they spend most of their waking hours on the job, "Why not," they say, "have a job with pleasant, congenial companions?" They feel it a must to work with people who have the same backgrounds, ideals, and goals as they. They consider it absolutely essential that they have this companionship on the job.

Some do not consider this an important factor. These persons view their job as a place to earn money or express themselves in their work. Companionship on the job is not particularly important to them.

What about you? Do you feel that during your interim dates and by the end of your planning horizon it would be a "must" for you to be working with a certain type of people? Or is this immaterial to you? Check the appropriate box.

*Freedom to Explore* (Creativity)—What about a job giving a

great deal of latitude in selecting assignments and in handling various tasks? Some people insist on this kind of job, which offers considerable opportunity for creativity. Is this a "must" for you? If so, check the box stating "Of Great Importance." If it is not, check the "Not Too Important" box.

How much freedom in your work do you feel it essential to have? For instance, in how much of your work must you be able to improvise and inject your own thinking? Try to evaluate this in a percentage figure and check the most suitable boxes.

Or perhaps freedom to explore is not a "must" for you. If so, check that box.

*Travel* (Amount of Time Out of Office)—Some people believe it mandatory that they have a job that will not keep them "tied down" to a desk day after day. They want a job that will, for example, allow them to spend a great part of their time out of the office.

Others feel the opposite. Record your "musts."

*Retirement Benefits*—Do you feel that if the job is right, you are not concerned with whether retirement benefits are part of the "package"? If this is your feeling, check the "Not-Too-Important" square.

Or do you feel it is a "must" that your job provide you with certain retirement benefits? If so, consider the following descriptions of retirement benefits (to be available at 65):

|  | *Per Week Benefits* |
|---|---|
| Few | $ 50 |
| Moderate | $100 |
| Many | $200 |

On the Must Goal list, check the box that corresponds to your "must" desires.

*Prestige of Job*—Some people feel they must have a job commanding considerable respect from others. They "must" be in a profession that, by tradition, is prestigious—such as law or medicine. On the other hand, some people do not care about job prestige. To them, it matters not whether they be a roughneck in an oilfield or a banker; they do not view a job as a means of impressing their fellow men.

How do you feel about a job and prestige? If you feel this is important, check the square of the type of people you feel *must* respect your job.

*Type of Business* (Profit or Nonprofit Firm)—What kind of business do you deem it absolutely necessary to be in at the end of your planning horizon? During the interim? Must you be working for a profit-oriented firm?

Or do you think it would be absolutely necessary for you to be aiding your fellow man by working for a nonprofit firm, such as a church or a university?

Or possibly it really does not matter. Check the proper box.

\*       \*       \*

Pause for a few minutes. Look back over the occupational goals you have just established. Do you think some other goals should be included? If so, write these goals in the space provided on page 54.

\*       \*       \*

*Financial Must Goals*

Below are a number of financial goals. Check the box representing what you would consider *absolutely essential* for your happiness during the interim and by the end of your planning horizon.

*Savings Accounts, Stocks, Bonds, Etc.*—This category includes values of stock options, pension funds, and other forms of savings, as well as amounts in regular savings accounts, stocks, and bonds. What is the least sum you think you *must* acquire during the interim and by the end of your planning horizon? Check the appropriate squares.

If such accumulations are really not mandatory as far as you are concerned, check the "Not-Too-Important" box.

*Home*—If you think it mandatory that you own your own home, decide what kind of house you would like to own. Although criteria other than monetary values may be used to describe a home, these do establish certain limits on the type of house you can acquire. Decide what the market value of your "must" house would be, and enter this figure in the appropriate places.

If this goal is not a "must" to you, check the "Not-Too-Important" box.

*Apartment or House* (Rental)—It may be that you do not feel it a must to own a home during part or all of your planning horizon. If so, this goal applies to you.

What type of rental unit do you feel you "must" live in? Decide on the rental value of this apartment (or house) and check the corresponding box.

*Vacation Home*—Perhaps owning a vacation home is a "must." If so, determine the market value of your "must" home and enter in the suitable boxes.

*Life Insurance*—Possibly you believe it mandatory to own a certain amount (face value) of life insurance. If so, write in the sum in the spaces provided.

*Other, Such as Autos, Boats, Airplanes, Etc.*—Are there any other "big-ticket" items you feel it mandatory that you own during—or by the end of—your planning horizon. If so, write in the names of items and their market values in the spaces provided on page 56.

### Self-Development Must Goals

Following are a number of goals relating to individual self-development. Determine and clarify those that are "musts" for your happiness during and by the end of your planning horizon.

*Physical Fitness*—Many people consider it a "must" to maintain (or improve) their physical fitness. Do you feel so? If so, what kind of physical fitness "must" you be in during and by the end of your planning horizon? Try to isolate certain measurable criteria.

Perhaps weight is one of these criteria. If so, record the desired weight.

Or it may be strength and/or endurance. In this case, specify minimum strength and/or endurance specifications, such as "x number of push-ups," or "to lift x pounds of weights," or "to be able to run the mile in x minutes."

Finally, you may have some other measurement. If so, record this in the space "Other." You may be interested in your posture. If that is the case, make a notation and sketch how you would like to look.

*Personal Skills*—What kind of skill(s) do you feel you *must* attain for your personal satisfaction? Suppose, for instance, you have a "must" desire to be a writer—not necessarily for money but for personal pleasure and fame. Your goal might be: to be a good writer—to have two short stories published by the *Atlantic Monthly* or equivalent. Or it might be to be an amateur actor. Then your goal might be: to be a good actor—to have had three lead parts in the Community Players' annual programs.

It could be that you feel it mandatory that you do some advanced study. *Note: Do not concern yourself here with additional formal education you might need for a job.* Rather, ask yourself,

"Is there any additional formal education I *must* have to be the kind of person I want to be?" If you feel you *must* have additional education, then write this in one of the allocated spaces. Write the kinds of skills and the degree of competence you hope to attain. This, incidentally, should be for both physical and mental skills.

*Vacations*—How much time during the year do you feel you must be free to take vacations? If you feel this is a *must,* specify the length of time, in days, per year. Also, approximate the amount of money you feel would be needed to give you the type of vacations you feel are absolutely necessary.

*Time With Hobbies*—How do you feel about hobbies, sports, etc.? Do you feel you "must" have a certain amount of time and/ or money to devote to your hobbies? If so, specify these hobbies. Then estimate the time and/or money required for these activities.

*             *             *

Stop. Examine the self-development Must Goals you have just established. Are there any other self-development Must Goals you think should be on this list? If so, write these goals in the space provided on page 58.

*             *             *

*Family Life Must Goals* (Husband and Wife Relationships)

*Marriage* (General)—Do you feel it a *must* that you be married during or by the end of your planning horizon? If your answer is "no" for your interim target dates and the terminal date of your planning horizon, then skip the remainder of this section and turn to pages 51 through 76.

If you feel it mandatory that sometime during or by the terminal date of your planning horizon you be married, complete the rest of this section.

*Note:* Establish goals for only the appropriate sections. If, for instance, you have no desire to marry until your second interim target date, and therefore you feel that marriage is not too important for your first interim target date, then set Must Goals only for the second interim target date and the planning horizon.

## Marriage (Attributes You Feel Your Spouse Must Possess)

*For the Unmarried*—One of the most important decisions you will make in your life is the selection of a marital partner. I am sure you have often thought about this, but do you know exactly what qualities and attributes you are looking for in a person with whom you are going to spend the rest of your life? "She's a good dancer" or "He dresses well" might be important for an evening or two, but probably not for a planning horizon that may extend to twenty years. Here are some suggested criteria for marital happiness that may help you focus in on exactly what you are seeking in marriage.

Circle those qualities you feel it mandatory that your partner possess.

*For the Married*—For you who are already married, examine this list for those qualities you feel you must refine or develop in your partner. (Of course some qualities on this list are inapplicable for a married person. Disregard these.)

*Note: Do not circle more than ten qualities.* You may find it tempting to circle all of the qualities listed on page 59. However, such a lengthy list of goals is usually self-defeating; it is too lengthy to be manageable.

*Marriage* (Time Together)—Do you feel you "must" be able to spend a certain number of evenings with your spouse every month? If so, how many? (Of course some months such time together might be impossible—so figure on the average.) Check the appropriate box.

*Marriage* (Communication)—Is it a "must" that you be able to communicate easily with your spouse? If so, what type of communicative relationship do you wish? Below are three examples. Select the type you feel best suits your desires; or specify the type of relationship you feel mandatory in the blank spaces provided.

*Type 1:* Restricted largely to optimistic, pleasant discussions. The communication would *not* include pessimistic thoughts or uncomplimentary statements that might make your spouse uncomfortable.

*Type 2:* Optimistic, pleasant discussions;

*and*

Also including topics that may be unpleasant, such as job difficulties, personal weaknesses, etc. Still, the communication is not totally open—you would not want to communicate some things.

*Type 3:* The communication would be "brutally frank"—even about deep inner feelings, even though they might be extremely uncomplimentary to your spouse and/or yourself.

*Marriage* (Sexual Adjustment)—"Must" your marriage have a certain level of sexual adjustment? If so, what type? Below are listed two types. Choose the most appropriate, or describe the relationship sought.

*Type 1:* Reserved, little discussion about sexual relationships, and even then, only on a superficial level. Infrequent sexual intercourse (less than once a week).

*Type 2:* Open; complete, frank discussion about sexual relationships. Frequent sexual intercourse.

*Marriage* (Social Life)—Do you consider it *absolutely* necessary that you and your spouse do a certain amount of entertaining? If so, what kind? Choose the most suitable type of the following (or improvise in the space provided).

*Type 1:* Social life restricted mostly to entertaining at home once or twice a month (small, informal groups), and an occasional dinner out. Club memberships limited to lodge or inexpensive country club.

*Type 2:* Entertaining at home on a more frequent basis and including a wider ranges of friends than Type 1; more evenings out. Club memberships include better lodges and/or country club.

*Type 3:* Similar to Type 2 above, only including expensive lodges and country club.

*Type 4:* Extensive and expensive entertaining at home and out, and memberships in the best clubs.

*Marriage* (Children)—Do you feel it a "must" to have children? If so, how many? Check the most suitable box, and circle whether you mean the number to be minimum (min.) or maximum (max.).

\* \* \*

Before you go any further, look back over your Marriage Must Goals. Do you feel that any other "Musts" should be included? Such additional goals might be: working together (professionally —such as Will and Ariel Durant), sharing of hobbies, sports, etc. If so, specify these Must Goals in the space provided on page 61.

\* \* \*

*Family Life Must Goals* (Parent-Child Relationship)

*Parent-Child Relationship* (General)—This kind of relationship, to be sure, presupposes that you will have children sometime during and prior to the end of your planning horizon. If, however, having children is not a must, then mark the "Not-Too-Important" boxes and turn to page 65.

However, if you feel it mandatory that sometime during or by the terminal date of your planning horizon you have children— and establish some sort of relationship with them—then check the appropriate "Mandatory" boxes and complete the remainder of this section.

*Parent-Child Relationship* (Attributes You Feel Your Children Must Possess)—Circle those attributes you feel it *mandatory* that your child(ren) possess.

*Note: Do not circle more than five qualities.* It may be enticing to circle more than five, but try to avoid doing so. Remember— lengthy lists tend to be self-defeating.

*Parent-Child Relationship* (Time Together)—You may believe it a "must" to be able to spend a certain number of evenings with your children every month. If so, how many? (Again, there may be some months when such time together might be impossible—so figure on the average.) Check the appropriate box.

*Parent-Child Relationship* (Communication)—Is it a "must" that you be able to communicate easily with your child(ren)? If so, what type of communicative relationship do you deem mandatory? Below are three examples. Select the type you feel best suits your desire (or improvise in the space allocated).

*Type 1:* Restricted largely to optimistic, pleasant discussions. The communication would *not* include pessimistic thoughts or uncomplimentary statements that might make your children uncomfortable.

*Type 2:* Optimistic, pleasant discussions;

*and*

Also including topics that may be unpleasant, such as

job difficulties, personal weaknesses, etc. Still the communication is not totally open—you would not want to communicate certain things.

*Type 3:* The communication would be "brutally frank"—even about deep inner feelings, even though they might be extremely uncomplimentary to your children and/or yourself.

\* \* \*

Stop. Examine your Family Life Must Goals (Parent-Child Relationship). Are there any others that should be included? If so, add these in the space allotted. (Some suggestions: sharing of hobbies, informal education, and formal education.)

\* \* \*

## Other Must Goals

Below are a number of "other" goals. Determine and clarify those that are "musts" for you.

*Close Relationship With Relatives* (Other Than Spouse or Children) *and/or Friends*—Do you have any relatives with whom you consider a close relationship a "must"? For example, you might have a brother with whom you feel you must have a close relationship. Or you may feel this way about your mother or father. If so, specify the person and check the appropriate type of relationship sought. Below are listed some suggested types. If you feel that none of these describes the relationship you are seeking, specify your desires in the appropriate places.

*Type 1:* This type of relationship would involve one or both of the following: occasional letter; occasional evening together.

*Type 2:* Similar to Type 1 above, but with letters and/or evening visits on a more frequent basis. Possibly an occasional weekend and/or vacation together.

*Type 3:* Similar to Type 2, plus planned weekends and vacations together.

*Participation in Community Affairs*—If it is mandatory that you participate in community affairs, decide on the type of involvement you wish. Check the corresponding type, or specify in the appropriate space.

*Type 1:*  To be involved in a minor project (such as soliciting for the Red Cross) on a more or less regular basis; and to take charge occasionally of a major project (such as being president of the P.-T.A.).

*Type 2:*  To be involved, on a regular basis, in a major project (example: president of the P.-T.A., member of the school board, political precinct chairman) and occasionally be involved in minor ones.

*Type 3:*  To be involved, on a regular basis, in two or more major projects.

*Social Life*—What kind of social life do you feel it mandatory to have? Note: Even if you have already specified the type of social life you would like to have with your spouse, still consider this section. You may feel it a must to have some specific kind of social life in addition to that specified for you and your spouse. For example, I know a person who considered it mandatory that, for social reasons, he become a member of the Union League Club of Philadelphia, a club designed almost exclusively for men.

If you feel you have certain social musts, specify them in the spaces provided.

*          *          *

Pause for a moment. Look over your Must-Goal List (pages 51 to 67). Does it contain everything you feel is absolutely necessary for you to have a successful life? If not, determine what other "musts" should be added and write in these additional Must Goals under the appropriate categories. Be sure that you clarify these goals.

## MUST-GOAL LIST

_____

Name

_____

Date

To be formally reviewed

_____ , 19____.

## OCCUPATION MUST GOALS

| CATEGORY | First Interim Target  Date _____ | Second Interim Target  Date _____ | Planning Horizon  Date _____ |
|---|---|---|---|
| MINIMUM ANNUAL SALARY | Not Too Important ☐  Mandatory (specify sum) $ _____ | Not Too Important ☐  Mandatory (specify sum) $ _____ | Not Too Important ☐  Mandatory (specify sum) $ _____ |
| TYPE OF EMPLOYMENT | Not Too Important ☐  Mandatory  Self-employed ☐  Work for Others ☐ | Not Too Important ☐  Mandatory  Self-employed ☐  Work for Others ☐ | Not Too Important ☐  Mandatory  Self-employed ☐  Work for Others ☐ |
| SIZE OF FIRM | Not Too Important ☐  Mandatory  Small ☐  Medium ☐  Large ☐ | Not Too Important ☐  Mandatory  Small ☐  Medium ☐  Large ☐ | Not Too Important ☐  Mandatory  Small ☐  Medium ☐  Large ☐ |
| GEOGRAPHIC AREA | Not Too Important ☐  Mandatory (specify location) _____ | Not Too Important ☐  Mandatory (specify location) _____ | Not Too Important ☐  Mandatory (specify location) _____ |
| TYPE OF WORK | Not Too Important ☐  Mandatory  Managerial ☐  Technical ☐ | Not Too Important ☐  Mandatory  Managerial ☐  Technical ☐ | Not Too Important ☐  Mandatory  Managerial ☐  Technical ☐ |

## OCCUPATION MUST GOALS (Continued)

| CATEGORY | First Interim Target Date ___ | Second Interim Target Date ___ | Planning Horizon Date ___ |
|---|---|---|---|
| TRAVEL (Away from Home) | Not Too Important □<br>Mandatory<br>Home Every Night □<br>Percent Away from Home □□□□□<br>　0–10<br>　11–20<br>　21–30<br>　Over 30 | Not Too Important □<br>Mandatory<br>Home Every Night □<br>Percent Away from Home □□□□□<br>　0–10<br>　11–20<br>　21–30<br>　Over 30 | Not Too Important □<br>Mandatory<br>Home Every Night □<br>Percent Away from Home □□□□□<br>　0–10<br>　11–20<br>　21–30<br>　Over 30 |
| SPEECHES AND PUBLIC APPEARANCES | Not Too Important □<br>Mandatory □□□□<br>　None<br>　Very Few<br>　Some<br>　Frequent | Not Too Important □<br>Mandatory □□□□<br>　None<br>　Very Few<br>　Some<br>　Frequent | Not Too Important □<br>Mandatory □□□□<br>　None<br>　Very Few<br>　Some<br>　Frequent |
| JOB SECURITY | Not Too Important □<br>Mandatory □□<br>　Very Stable<br>　Moderately Stable | Not Too Important □<br>Mandatory □□<br>　Very Stable<br>　Moderately Stable | Not Too Important □<br>Mandatory □□<br>　Very Stable<br>　Moderately Stable |
| JOB FLEXIBILITY | Not Too Important □<br>Mandatory □<br>Fixed Schedule<br>Moderately Flexible □<br>　Schedule<br>Extremely Flexible □<br>　Schedule | Not Too Important □<br>Mandatory □<br>Fixed Schedule<br>Moderately Flexible □<br>　Schedule<br>Extremely Flexible □<br>　Schedule | Not Too Important □<br>Mandatory □<br>Fixed Schedule<br>Moderately Flexible □<br>　Schedule<br>Extremely Flexible □<br>　Schedule |

## OCCUPATION MUST GOALS (Continued)

| CATEGORY | First Interim Target<br>Date _____ | Second Interim Target<br>Date _____ | Planning Horizon<br>Date _____ |
|---|---|---|---|
| WORKING ENVIRONMENT (Physical) | Not Too Important □<br>Mandatory<br>Modern, Well Appointed □<br>Lavish, Extravagant □ | Not Too Important □<br>Mandatory<br>Modern, Well Appointed □<br>Lavish, Extravagant □ | Not Too Important □<br>Mandatory<br>Modern, Well Appointed □<br>Lavish, Extravagant □ |
| WORKING ENVIRONMENT (Companion Relationships) | Not Too Important □<br>Mandatory<br>Laborers □□<br>Foremen □<br>Beginning Management and Professionals □<br>Middle Management and Professionals □<br>Top Management and Professionals □ | Not Too Important □<br>Mandatory<br>Laborers □□<br>Foremen □<br>Beginning Management and Professionals □<br>Middle Management and Professionals □<br>Top Management and Professionals □ | Not Too Important □<br>Mandatory<br>Laborers □□<br>Foremen □<br>Beginning Management and Professionals □<br>Middle Management and Professionals □<br>Top Management and Professionals □ |
| FREEDOM TO EXPLORE | Not Too Important □<br>Mandatory<br>0-10 Percent □□□□<br>11-20 Percent<br>21-40 Percent<br>Over 40 Percent | Not Too Important □<br>Mandatory<br>0-10 Percent □□□□<br>11-20 Percent<br>21-40 Percent<br>Over 40 Percent | Not Too Important □<br>Mandatory<br>0-10 Percent □□□□<br>11-20 Percent<br>21-40 Percent<br>Over 40 Percent |
| TRAVEL (Amount of Time out of Office) | Not Too Important □<br>Mandatory<br>Stay in Office<br>Percent Out of Office □□□□□□<br>0-10<br>11-20<br>21-30<br>Over 30 | Not Too Important □<br>Mandatory<br>Stay in Office<br>Percent Out of Office □□□□□□<br>0-10<br>11-20<br>21-30<br>Over 30 | Not Too Important □<br>Mandatory<br>Stay in Office<br>Percent Out of Office □□□□□□<br>0-10<br>11-20<br>21-30<br>Over 30 |

## OCCUPATION MUST GOALS (Continued)

| CATEGORY | First Interim Target<br>Date _____ | Second Interim Target<br>Date _____ | Planning Horizon<br>Date _____ |
|---|---|---|---|
| RETIREMENT BENEFITS | Not Too Important ☐<br>Mandatory<br>Few ☐<br>Moderate ☐<br>Many ☐ | Not Too Important ☐<br>Mandatory<br>Few ☐<br>Moderate ☐<br>Many ☐ | Not Too Important ☐<br>Mandatory<br>Few ☐<br>Moderate ☐<br>Many ☐ |
| PRESTIGE OF JOB | Not Too Important ☐<br>Mandatory<br>Laborers ☐<br>Foremen ☐<br>Beginning Management and Professionals ☐<br>Middle Management and Professionals ☐<br>Top Management and Professionals ☐ | Not Too Important ☐<br>Mandatory<br>Laborers ☐<br>Foremen ☐<br>Beginning Management and Professionals ☐<br>Middle Management and Professionals ☐<br>Top Management and Professionals ☐ | Not Too Important ☐<br>Mandatory<br>Laborers ☐<br>Foremen ☐<br>Beginning Management and Professionals ☐<br>Middle Management and Professionals ☐<br>Top Management and Professionals ☐ |
| TYPE OF BUSINESS<br>(Non-profit--Profit Firm) | Not Too Important ☐<br>Mandatory<br>Profit-oriented ☐<br>Nonprofit-oriented ☐ | Not Too Important ☐<br>Mandatory<br>Profit-oriented ☐<br>Nonprofit-oriented ☐ | Not Too Important ☐<br>Mandatory<br>Profit-oriented ☐<br>Nonprofit-oriented ☐ |
| OTHER | | | |

## FINANCIAL MUST GOALS

| CATEGORY | First Interim Target Date _____ | Second Interim Target Date _____ | Planning Horizon Date _____ |
|---|---|---|---|
| SAVINGS ACCOUNTS, STOCKS, BONDS, ETC. | ☐ Not Too Important<br>Mandatory (Specify Sum) $ _____ | ☐ Not Too Important<br>Mandatory (Specify Sum) $ _____ | ☐ Not Too Important<br>Mandatory (Specify Sum) $ _____ |
| HOME | ☐ Not Too Important<br>Mandatory (Specify Market Value) $ _____ | ☐ Not Too Important<br>Mandatory (Specify Market Value) $ _____ | ☐ Not Too Important<br>Mandatory (Specify Market Value) $ _____ |
| APARTMENT OR HOUSE (Rental) | ☐ Not Too Important<br>Mandatory (Specify Rental Value)<br>☐ Under $150<br>☐ $150 - $249<br>☐ $250 - $349<br>☐ $350 - $500<br>Over $500 (Specify) _____ | ☐ Not Too Important<br>Mandatory (Specify Rental Value)<br>☐ Under $150<br>☐ $150 - $249<br>☐ $250 - $349<br>☐ $350 - $500<br>Over $500 (Specify) _____ | ☐ Not Too Important<br>Mandatory (Specify Rental Value)<br>☐ Under $150<br>☐ $150 - $249<br>☐ $250 - $349<br>☐ $350 - $500<br>Over $500 (Specify) _____ |
| VACATION HOME | ☐ Not Too Important<br>Mandatory (Specify Market Value) $ _____ | ☐ Not Too Important<br>Mandatory (Specify Market Value) $ _____ | ☐ Not Too Important<br>Mandatory (Specify Market Value) $ _____ |
| LIFE INSURANCE | ☐ Not Too Important<br>Mandatory (Specify Face Value) $ _____ | ☐ Not Too Important<br>Mandatory (Specify Face Value) $ _____ | ☐ Not Too Important<br>Mandatory (Specify Face Value) $ _____ |

## FINANCIAL MUST GOALS (Continued)

| CATEGORY | First Interim Target | Second Interim Target | Planning Horizon |
|---|---|---|---|
| | Date _____ | Date _____ | Date _____ |
| OTHER, SUCH AS AUTOS, BOATS, AIRPLANES, ETC. <br><br>(List each item separately by description and value) | Item _____ <br> Market Value $ _____ | Item _____ <br> Market Value $ _____ | Item _____ <br> Market Value $ _____ |
| | Item _____ <br> Market Value $ _____ | Item _____ <br> Market Value $ _____ | Item _____ <br> Market Value $ _____ |
| | Item _____ <br> Market Value $ _____ | Item _____ <br> Market Value $ _____ | Item _____ <br> Market Value $ _____ |
| | Item _____ <br> Market Value $ _____ | Item _____ <br> Market Value $ _____ | Item _____ <br> Market Value $ _____ |
| | Item _____ <br> Market Value $ _____ | Item _____ <br> Market Value $ _____ | Item _____ <br> Market Value $ _____ |
| | Item _____ <br> Market Value $ _____ | Item _____ <br> Market Value $ _____ | Item _____ <br> Market Value $ _____ |
| | Item _____ <br> Market Value $ _____ | Item _____ <br> Market Value $ _____ | Item _____ <br> Market Value $ _____ |
| | Item _____ <br> Market Value $ _____ | Item _____ <br> Market Value $ _____ | Item _____ <br> Market Value $ _____ |

## SELF-DEVELOPMENT MUST GOALS

| CATEGORY | First Interim Target<br>Date _____ | Second Interim Target<br>Date _____ | Planning Horizon<br>Date _____ |
|---|---|---|---|
| PHYSICAL FITNESS | Not Too Important ☐<br>Mandatory<br>  Measurements:<br>    Weight _____<br>    Strength (Specify<br>    Measurement) _____<br>    _____<br>  Endurance (Specify<br>  Measurement) _____<br>    _____<br>  Other _____<br>    _____ | Not Too Important ☐<br>Mandatory<br>  Measurements:<br>    Weight _____<br>    Strength (Specify<br>    Measurement) _____<br>    _____<br>  Endurance (Specify<br>  Measurement) _____<br>    _____<br>  Other _____<br>    _____ | Not Too Important ☐<br>Mandatory<br>  Measurements:<br>    Weight _____<br>    Strength (Specify<br>    Measurement) _____<br>    _____<br>  Endurance (Specify<br>  Measurement) _____<br>    _____<br>  Other _____<br>    _____ |
| PERSONAL SKILLS | Not Too Important ☐<br>Mandatory<br>  Skill _____<br>  Measurement of<br>  Proficiency: _____<br>    _____<br>  Skill _____<br>  Measurement of<br>  Proficiency: _____<br>    _____ | Not Too Important ☐<br>Mandatory<br>  Skill _____<br>  Measurement of<br>  Proficiency: _____<br>    _____<br>  Skill _____<br>  Measurement of<br>  Proficiency: _____<br>    _____ | Not Too Important ☐<br>Mandatory<br>  Skill _____<br>  Measurement of<br>  Proficiency: _____<br>    _____<br>  Skill _____<br>  Measurement of<br>  Proficiency: _____<br>    _____ |

## SELF-DEVELOPMENT MUST GOALS (Continued)

| CATEGORY | First Interim Target Date _____ | Second Interim Target Date _____ | Planning Horizon Date _____ |
|---|---|---|---|
| VACATIONS | ☐ Not Too Important<br>Mandatory<br>Time (Specify Days per Year) _____<br>Cost (per Year) $_____ | ☐ Not Too Important<br>Mandatory<br>Time (Specify Days per Year) _____<br>Cost (per Year) $_____ | ☐ Not Too Important<br>Mandatory<br>Time (Specify Days per Year) _____<br>Cost (per Year) $_____ |
| TIME WITH HOBBIES | ☐ Not Too Important<br>Mandatory<br>Hobby _____<br>Time Required _____<br>Money Required (per Year) $_____<br>Hobby _____<br>Time Required _____<br>Money Required (per Year) $_____<br>Hobby _____<br>Time Required _____<br>Money Required (per Year) $_____ | ☐ Not Too Important<br>Mandatory<br>Hobby _____<br>Time Required _____<br>Money Required (per Year) $_____<br>Hobby _____<br>Time Required _____<br>Money Required (per Year) $_____<br>Hobby _____<br>Time Required _____<br>Money Required (per Year) $_____ | ☐ Not Too Important<br>Mandatory<br>Hobby _____<br>Time Required _____<br>Money Required (per Year) $_____<br>Hobby _____<br>Time Required._____<br>Money Required (per Year) $_____<br>Hobby _____<br>Time Required _____<br>Money Required (per Year) $_____ |
| OTHER | | | |

FAMILY LIFE MUST GOALS (HUSBAND–WIFE RELATIONSHIPS)

| CATEGORY | First Interim Target | Second Interim Target | Planning Horizon |
|---|---|---|---|
| | Date _____ | Date _____ | Date _____ |
| MARRIAGE (General) | Not Too Important ☐ <br> Mandatory ☐ | Not Too Important ☐ <br> Mandatory ☐ | Not Too Important ☐ <br> Mandatory ☐ |

NOTE: If, for MARRIAGE (General) you checked "Not Too Important" for all three planning dates, then skip to page 65.

**MARRIAGE (Attributes You Feel Your Spouse Must Possess)**

Circle those attributes you feel it mandatory that your spouse possess BUT NOTE--circle no more than 10 attributes.

| | | |
|---|---|---|
| trust | similar sex drives | wealth |
| confidence | attractiveness | ambition |
| understanding | courteousness | mutual friendships |
| honesty | tactfulness | mutual admiration |
| reliability | charm | mutuality of interests and |
| maturity | sense of humor | skills |
| patience | intelligence | similar goals |
| social position | health | similar background |
| ability to project a | flexibility | similar social class, economic |
| social image | similar hobbies | status |

MARRIAGE (Attributes You Feel Your Spouse Must Possess):
- First Interim Target: Not Too Important ☐   ☐☐☐☐☐
- Second Interim Target: Not Too Important ☐   ☐☐☐☐☐
- Planning Horizon: Not Too Important ☐   ☐☐☐☐☐

**MARRIAGE (Time Together)**

| | First Interim Target | Second Interim Target | Planning Horizon |
|---|---|---|---|
| | Not Too Important ☐ | Not Too Important ☐ | Not Too Important ☐ |
| | Mandatory <br> Evenings per Month | Mandatory <br> Evenings per Month | Mandatory <br> Evenings per Month |
| | 1 - 5 | 1 - 5 | 1 - 5 |
| | 6 - 10 | 6 - 10 | 6 - 10 |
| | 11 - 15 | 11 - 15 | 11 - 15 |
| | 16 - 20 | 16 - 20 | 16 - 20 |
| | 21 - 25 | 21 - 25 | 21 - 25 |
| | 26 - 30 | 26 - 30 | 26 - 30 |

## FAMILY LIFE MUST GOALS (HUSBAND-WIFE RELATIONSHIPS) (Continued)

| | First Interim Target<br>Date ___ | Second Interim Target<br>Date ___ | Planning Horizon<br>Date ___ |
|---|---|---|---|
| MARRIAGE<br>(Communication) | Not Too Important ☐   ☐☐☐<br>Mandatory<br>Type 1<br>Type 2<br>Type 3<br>Other (Specify) ___ | Not Too Important ☐   ☐☐☐<br>Mandatory<br>Type 1<br>Type 2<br>Type 3<br>Other (Specify) ___ | Not Too Important ☐   ☐☐☐<br>Mandatory<br>Type 1<br>Type 2<br>Type 3<br>Other (Specify) ___ |
| MARRIAGE<br>(Sexual Adjustment) | Not Too Important ☐   ☐☐<br>Mandatory<br>Type 1<br>Type 2<br>Other (Specify) ___ | Not Too Important ☐   ☐☐<br>Mandatory<br>Type 1<br>Type 2<br>Other (Specify) ___ | Not Too Important ☐   ☐☐<br>Mandatory<br>Type 1<br>Type 2<br>Other (Specify) ___ |
| MARRIAGE (Social Life) | Not Too Important ☐   ☐☐☐☐<br>Mandatory<br>Type 1<br>Type 2<br>Type 3<br>Type 4<br>Other (Specify) ___ | Not Too Important ☐   ☐☐☐☐<br>Mandatory<br>Type 1<br>Type 2<br>Type 3<br>Type 4<br>Other (Specify) ___ | Not Too Important ☐   ☐☐☐☐<br>Mandatory<br>Type 1<br>Type 2<br>Type 3<br>Type 4<br>Other (Specify) ___ |

FAMILY LIFE MUST GOALS (HUSBAND–WIFE RELATIONSHIPS) (Continued)

| CATEGORY | First Interim Target | Second Interim Target | Planning Horizon |
|---|---|---|---|
| | Date _____ | Date _____ | Date _____ |
| MARRIAGE (Children) | ☐ Not Too Important<br>Mandatory: Number of<br>Children<br>1 ___ min. ___ max.<br>2 ___ min. ___ max.<br>3 ___ min. ___ max.<br>4 ___ min. ___ max.<br>Over 4 ___ min. ___ max.<br>(Specify)<br>☐☐☐☐☐ | ☐ Not Too Important<br>Mandatory: Number of<br>Children<br>1 ___ min. ___ max.<br>2 ___ min. ___ max.<br>3 ___ min. ___ max.<br>4 ___ min. ___ max.<br>Over 4 ___ min. ___ max.<br>(Specify)<br>☐☐☐☐☐ | ☐ Not Too Important<br>Mandatory: Number of<br>Children<br>1 ___ min. ___ max.<br>2 ___ min. ___ max.<br>3 ___ min. ___ max.<br>4 ___ min. ___ max.<br>Over 4 ___ min. ___ max.<br>(Specify)<br>☐☐☐☐☐ |
| OTHER (Specify) | | | |

## FAMILY LIFE MUST GOALS (PARENT-CHILD RELATIONSHIPS)

| CATEGORY | First Interim Target<br>Date _____ | Second Interim Target<br>Date _____ | Planning Horizon<br>Date _____ |
|---|---|---|---|
| PARENT-CHILD RELATIONSHIP (General) | ☐ Not Too Important<br>☐ Mandatory | ☐ Not Too Important<br>☐ Mandatory | ☐ Not Too Important<br>☐ Mandatory |

NOTE: If, for PARENT-CHILD RELATIONSHIP (General), you checked "Not Too Important" for all three planning dates, then skip to page 65.

| CATEGORY | First Interim Target | Second Interim Target | Planning Horizon |
|---|---|---|---|
| PARENT-CHILD RELATIONSHIP (Attributes you Feel Your Children Must Possess) | Circle those attributes you feel mandatory that your child possess. BUT NOTE-- circle those no more than five attributes.<br><br>creativity    willingness to accept change<br>analytical ability    courtesy<br>sociability    tactfulness<br>sincerity    obedience<br>patience    independence<br>honesty    skill at sports | | |
| | ☐ Not Too Important<br>☐ Mandatory<br>☐☐☐☐☐☐ | ☐ Not Too Important<br>☐ Mandatory<br>☐☐☐☐☐☐ | ☐ Not Too Important<br>☐ Mandatory<br>☐☐☐☐☐☐ |
| PARENT-CHILD RELATIONSHIP (Time Together) | ☐ Not Too Important<br>☐ Mandatory<br>Evenings per Month<br>1 - 5<br>6 - 10<br>11 - 15<br>16 - 20<br>21 - 25<br>26 - 30 | ☐ Not Too Important<br>☐ Mandatory<br>Evenings per Month<br>1 - 5<br>6 - 10<br>11 - 15<br>16 - 20<br>21 - 25<br>26 - 30 | ☐ Not Too Important<br>☐ Mandatory<br>Evenings per Month<br>1 - 5<br>6 - 10<br>11 - 15<br>16 - 20<br>21 - 25<br>26 - 30 |

## FAMILY LIFE MUST GOALS (PARENT-CHILD RELATIONSHIP) (Continued)

| | First Interim Target<br>Date ___ | Second Interim Target<br>Date ___ | Planning Horizon<br>Date ___ |
|---|---|---|---|
| PARENT–CHILD RELA-<br>TIONSHIP<br>(Communication) | Not Too Important ☐<br>Mandatory<br>Type 1 ☐<br>Type 2 ☐<br>Type 3 ☐<br>Other (Specify) ___<br>___<br>___<br>___<br>___ | Not Too Important ☐<br>Mandatory<br>Type 1 ☐<br>Type 2 ☐<br>Type 3 ☐<br>Other (Specify) ___<br>___<br>___<br>___<br>___ | Not Too Important ☐<br>Mandatory<br>Type 1 ☐<br>Type 2 ☐<br>Type 3 ☐<br>Other (Specify) ___<br>___<br>___<br>___<br>___ |
| OTHER (Specify) | | | |

OTHER MUST GOALS

| CATEGORY | First Interim Target<br>Date _____ | Second Interim Target<br>Date _____ | Planning Horizon<br>Date _____ |
|---|---|---|---|
| CLOSE RELATIONSHIP WITH RELATIVES (Other Than Spouse or Children) and/or Friends) | Not Too Important ☐<br>Mandatory<br>Person_____<br>Relationship Sought ☐☐☐<br>Type 1<br>Type 2<br>Type 3<br>Other_____<br>_____<br>Person_____<br>Relationship Sought ☐☐☐<br>Type 1<br>Type 2<br>Type 3<br>Other_____<br>_____<br>Person_____<br>Relationship Sought ☐☐☐<br>Type 1<br>Type 2<br>Type 3<br>Other_____ | Not Too Important ☐<br>Mandatory<br>Person_____<br>Relationship Sought ☐☐☐<br>Type 1<br>Type 2<br>Type 3<br>Other_____<br>_____<br>Person_____<br>Relationship Sought ☐☐☐<br>Type 1<br>Type 2<br>Type 3<br>Other_____<br>_____<br>Person_____<br>Relationship Sought ☐☐☐<br>Type 1<br>Type 2<br>Type 3<br>Other_____ | Not Too Important ☐<br>Mandatory<br>Person_____<br>Relationship Sought ☐☐☐<br>Type 1<br>Type 2<br>Type 3<br>Other_____<br>_____<br>Person_____<br>Relationship Sought ☐☐☐<br>Type 1<br>Type 2<br>Type 3<br>Other_____<br>_____<br>Person_____<br>Relationship Sought ☐☐☐<br>Type 1<br>Type 2<br>Type 3<br>Other_____ |

## OTHER MUST GOALS (Continued)

| CATEGORY | First Interim Target | Second Interim Target | Planning Horizon |
|---|---|---|---|
| | Date _____ | Date _____ | Date _____ |
| CLOSE RELATIONSHIP WITH RELATIVES (Other Than Spouse or Children) and/or Friends) | Not Too Important ☐ | Not Too Important ☐ | Not Too Important ☐ |
| | Mandatory Person _____ | Mandatory Person _____ | Mandatory Person _____ |
| | Relationship Sought ☐☐☐ ☐☐ <br> Type 1 <br> Type 2 <br> Type 3 <br> Other _____ | Relationship Sought ☐☐☐ <br> Type 1 <br> Type 2 <br> Type 3 <br> Other _____ | Relationship Sought ☐☐☐ <br> Type 1 <br> Type 2 <br> Type 3 <br> Other _____ |
| | Person _____ | Person _____ | Person _____ |
| | Relationship Sought ☐☐☐ <br> Type 1 <br> Type 2 <br> Type 3 <br> Other _____ | Relationship Sought ☐☐☐ <br> Type 1 <br> Type 2 <br> Type 3 <br> Other _____ | Relationship Sought ☐☐☐ <br> Type 1 <br> Type 2 <br> Type 3 <br> Other _____ |
| | Person _____ | Person _____ | Person _____ |
| | Relationship Sought ☐☐☐ <br> Type 1 <br> Type 2 <br> Type 3 <br> Other _____ | Relationship Sought ☐☐☐ <br> Type 1 <br> Type 2 <br> Type 3 <br> Other _____ | Relationship Sought ☐☐☐ <br> Type 1 <br> Type 2 <br> Type 3 <br> Other _____ |

## OTHER MUST GOALS (Continued)

| | First Interim Target<br>Date _____ | Second Interim Target<br>Date _____ | Planning Horizon<br>Date _____ |
|---|---|---|---|
| PARTICIPATION IN COMMUNITY AFFAIRS | Not Too Important ☐<br>Mandatory<br>  Type 1 ☐<br>  Type 2 ☐<br>  Type 3 ☐<br>  Other (Specify) ____ | Not Too Important ☐<br>Mandatory<br>  Type 1 ☐<br>  Type 2 ☐<br>  Type 3 ☐<br>  Other (Specify) ____ | Not Too Important ☐<br>Mandatory<br>  Type 1 ☐<br>  Type 2 ☐<br>  Type 3 ☐<br>  Other (Specify) ____ |
| SOCIAL LIFE | Not Too Important ☐<br>Mandatory<br>  Specify: | Not Too Important ☐<br>Mandatory<br>  Specify: | Not Too Important ☐<br>Mandatory<br>  Specify: |

\*          \*          \*

I suggest you stop for now. The next step will be a critical re-examination of your Must Goals. Why not set your alarm for fifteen minutes earlier and do this tomorrow morning while your mind is fresh?

\*          \*          \*

*Critical Appraisal of Your Must Goals*
*(Time Required: 15 minutes)*

Now, reexamine your Must-Goal List. Ask yourself these questions:

1. Does the thought of obtaining these goals make me enthused?
   (If it does not, I suggest you go back and reestablish your goals, and while so doing, think in terms of, "What will it take to give me a zest for life?" *Do not proceed until you have established exciting goals.*)
2. Does your Must-Goal List give an accurate description of all your "must" desires in life?
   (If not, then structure your list until it does.)

If you can answer both of the above questions in the affirmative, proceed to Chapter IV.

## Must Goal Reconciliation
## (Time Required: 1½ hours)

Before you start to develop plans for attaining your goals, a good procedure is to make sure they are reconcilable.

This step is important for many reasons. Among the most salient are:

1. You may find—through this reconciliation—that your minimum annual income requirements might need to be increased appreciably in order for you to meet other Must Goals.

For instance, you may have established Must Goals: a. to be living in a $40,000 home; b. to belong to an expensive country club; c. to take vacations costing $1,500 a year; and d. to have a type of social life demanding a considerable sum of money. On the other hand, your Minimum Annual Salary Must Goal might have been $12,000, not enough to meet the needs of these requirements. During the reconciliation, then, the Annual Salary Must Goal should be increased.

2. The second reason for reconciling your goals is that you may have made demands on your time that cannot be met.

Here is an example: A person may have set Must Goals to have a job entailing a considerable amount of travel—say 30 percent of the time away from home. Yet he established a Must Goal to spend at least twenty evenings a month at home with his family, five evenings with friends and six evenings working on community affairs. To make his Must Goals operational, some adjustment will have to be made.

3. Finally, some goals may have consequences of which you might not be aware.

In this chapter you will:

- examine further aspects of certain goals.
- check your goals to see if they are operational and make necessary corrections.

*     *     *

Further aspects of selected goals are discussed below.[1] Refer to your Must-Goal Lists while reading through the following comments, and make any changes in these lists that seem appropriate.

*Minimum Annual Salary—For high-school graduates.* The starting salary for jobs in industry is approximately $5,500 (slightly higher in sales). The trend today seems to be to reserve management positions for persons with college degrees. Consequently, most high-school graduates will find that their yearly wages will probably peak out somewhere between $10,000 and $20,000 (in 1969 dollars). The length of time it will take to reach this figure will depend upon many variables, such as the type of occupation, firm, and industry, and, of course, the individual's own abilities and willingness to acquire additional education.

Here is an example of what you might expect if you decided to enter—and qualified for apprenticeship in—the sheet-metal trade. You would start at approximately $2.75 an hour (Philadelphia area rates). Every six months you would be eligible for a $.32-an-hour raise. During the fourth year, however, your raises would be accelerated, and by the end of the fourth year you would be making about $6.50 an hour, plus fringe benefits amounting to approximately $.50 an hour. (Actually, your wage rate would approximate $7.00 an hour by the end of the fourth year because of union contracts, which call for yearly accelerations.) After the fourth year, however, your earnings would stabilize. Your hopes for increased annual income would be dependent upon:

- increases in wages due to raises in union scale.
- promotion to a foreman's position.

---

[1] It was felt that there was no need to discuss further some of the goals on the Must-Goal Lists. To provide continuity, however, they are mentioned and designated by an asterisk.

- going into business for yourself—becoming an independent contractor.
- revenues from savings or outside investments.

*Minimum Annual Salary—For graduates holding a bachelor degree,* the starting salary for jobs in industry is somewhere between $6,000 and $9,000, the median being $7,500. On-the-job salary increases depend not only upon you, but on other factors. Three of the most basic are:

### Type of Industry or Business

Although the starting salaries may be approximately equal among different industries and businesses, the salaries received by the chief executives have been found to vary widely, depending upon the type of firm or industry. Since other executive salaries are usually determined on a percentage basis of the chief executive's, a person working for a firm in an industry that typically pays its chief executive a high salary has a better chance to receive greater salary increases than one working in an industry that pays its chief executive a relatively low salary. *Business Management* (January 1968, p. 32) reports executive compensation, by type of industry and business; see page 72.

### Growth of the Firm

The more rapid rate of growth, the better are your chances for "accelerated" advancement.

### Risks Involved

If the job is in an industry in which the probability of being fired for inefficiency is high, this industry often offers opportunities for rapid advancement.

*Type of Employment*—(Read only if you checked "Self-employed.") You will probably need investment and operating capital. In addition, you will have to consider other implications.
Here are three examples:

1. *Job Flexibility*—If your business is small, you may find that it will be impractical for you to delegate many tasks.

*Executive Compensation, 1968, in High- and Low-Paying Industries*

TABLE 1

| Industry | Salary | Total Compensation | Industry | Salary | Total Compensation |
|---|---|---|---|---|---|
| Aerospace | I | III | Hospitals | V | V |
| Automotive Supplier | I | I | Instruments | IV | III |
| Automobile and Truck | II | II | Leather | III | II |
| Banks | III | IV | Life and Group Insurance | II | III |
| Beverage | III | IV | Machinery | IV | IV |
| Business Supplies and Equipment | III | III | Metals | II | III |
| Business Machinery and Equipment | I | I | Paper | III | V |
| Casualty Insurance | V | V | Petroleum and Gas Utilities | I | III |
| Chemicals | IV | IV | Pharmaceutical | III | II |
| Construction | III | II | Printing and Publishing | I | I |
| Education | V | V | Rubber | IV | IV |
| Electrical and Electronic | II | III | Textile | II | II |
| Fabricated Metal Products | III | III | Tobacco | II | I |
| Food | IV | IV | Tools and Hardware | III | I |
| Furniture | III | IV | Transportation | IV | V |
| Glass | III | III | Utilities | V | V |
| Government | V | V | Wholesale and Retail | V | V |

This might demand your presence at your place of business on a "fixed" basis.

2. *Vacations*—For the same reason, you may find it impractical to take vacations when you feel the need.

3. *Retirement Benefits*—You will have to establish your own retirement fund. This will demand that a greater percentage of your earnings go into savings.

*Size of Firm*—Small and medium-sized firms are more likely to be "family-owned" and controlled than are large firms; as a result, the top management posts are more likely to be "reserved" for members of the family.

*Geographic Area*—Although discussion of this might be a bit premature, if you have a "must" to live in a certain area, give some consideration to: banks, law firms, local government, investment companies, utilities, and educational institutions. These are some of the industries that "tend to stay put" in a given location.

On the other hand, if you work for a firm that is national and/or international in scope, plan to be transferred to different areas from time to time. The transfers are usually associated with a promotion (an opportunity opens up in another area), and a person who refuses to move is usually denied the promotion. Although the amount of movement varies widely, it is not uncommon for a person to be transferred every three years.

*Type of Work*—Usually the very high-paying jobs are those involving management of others. There is—generally speaking—a paucity of technical jobs paying over $25,000 a year. Some of these are: lawyers, doctors, and various types of salesmen (insurance, stock brokers, manufacturer's representatives, among others). The basic point still stands, however.

For example, many engineers and chemists, after a few years on the job, find that their salary has reached a plateau. In order to increase their earnings appreciably they move into management. Often this involves acquiring an M.B.A. (Master of Business Administration) degree.

*Travel* (Away from Home)—At certain times in one's life extensive travel has adverse effects. Many young married couples, just starting a family, find it hard to manage if the husband is away from home for a considerable amount of time.

For example: The wife is at home with young children, and as delightful as one's children are, after ten hours a day—plus night feedings—they do get a little tiring. She lacks adult companionship. And she has the house to take care of. There are many things she cannot do, so when the husband comes home, he has to fix the faucets, mow the lawn, pay certain bills, etc. Thus, even though he might be at home for the weekend, his time is often filled with "non-fun" activities. This type of relationship, over a period of time, can do much to cause a marriage to falter.

After the children are older and in school, and the wife has more "freedom," extensive travel on the part of the husband is often more bearable—as far as the spouse is concerned.

*Speeches and Public Appearances*—Many people do not like to give speeches. However, as one progresses into the upper echelons of management, this type of activity becomes more necessary.

Then, too, presentations are often required even of scientists and technicians.

(An engineer, working for a large computer manufacturer, was project manager on a development program. He presented a progress report to top management. Although the project was "in good shape," he was replaced as project manager. His oral presentation was so poor that the top management lost confidence in his ability.)

*Job Security*—If you feel you "must" have job security, you should be aware that this "benefit" may mean that your advancement within the organization will be slow. An organization may be depicted as a pyramid to the top. In some organizations—in which high-level performance is expected of individuals *or else*— a slicing-off at the sides occurs. This procedure allows a more rapid ascension for those who can and do produce. Unless some "weeding out" is done, your rise within the organization will be dependent upon: a) the death or retirement of those in echelons above you, or b) growth of the company.

Furthermore, in a "high-security" firm, managers tend to become complacent. Under these conditions it is often difficult to initiate change, and as a result, the middle-level managers are often frustrated because of inability to get things done.

Besides, no company can guarantee you complete security. Management—and ownership—can change, and so can the policies concerning employee retention.

Actually, the greatest security one can acquire is through self-development—by being able to do tasks better than others.

*Job Flexibility*—Most managers find that they do have a certain amount of flexibility in their schedule, yet they also find that they are often required to work nights and weekends in periods of crisis.

*Working Environment* (Physical)*

*Working Environment* (Companion Relationship)*

*Freedom to Explore**

*Travel* (Amount of Time Out of Office)*

*Retirement Benefits**

*Prestige of Job*—If you checked this as being important, then, to be safe, make sure your salary matches the salary received by members of the group whose respect you want. Salary is just one criterion of success—yet it is a very important one.

Many people are deluded into thinking they will attain a great deal of respect from all people by becoming a "public servant,"

---

* The asterisk denotes "no further comment."

such as a teacher. Yet many top-level managers do not consider teachers to be on their "level."

Perhaps it depends upon what you mean by respect. True, everyone should respect his fellow man to some degree and for certain things. But if you want a person to respect you as a professional equal, then the complexity of your profession should match the complexity of his. Again, salary is only one measurement, but it is a pretty good one!

Here is a rough scale to use:

|  | *Annual Salary* |
|---|---|
| Beginning management and professionals | $ 8,000 to $16,000 |
| Middle management and professionals | $16,000 to $35,000 |
| Top management and professionals | more than $35,000 |

*Type of Business* *

*Savings Accounts, Stocks, Bonds, etc.* *

*Home* *

*Apartment or House (Rental)* *

*Vacation Home* *

*Life Insurance*—Regardless of your present goals, a fact to remember is that eventually most people do get married and do raise a family. Except for the financially independent, most people need the protection a well-designed life-insurance program can provide. Consequently, if you have not already started such a plan, you should give it serious consideration.

Four basic reasons are:

1. A person's health may deteriorate—from a heart condition, for instance—and as a result, make him uninsurable. Unlikely as this might seem to you now, *it could happen.*

2. It offers a form of forced saving. Many graduates find it

* The asterisk denotes "no further comment."

difficult to save money. A definite commitment—such as a life-insurance program—often provides the needed incentive.

3. An insurance policy can be a source of capital. Practically all life-insurance programs have a provision whereby the policyholder may borrow against the cash value of the policy. The interest rates charged for these loans are usually far less than what one would have to pay on the open market.

4. Insurance rates are lower when one is younger.

*Other, Such as Autos, Boats, Airplanes, Etc.**

*Physical Fitness**

*Personal Skills**

*Vacations**

*Time With Hobbies**

*Marriage* (General) *

*Marriage* (Attributes You Feel Your Spouse Must Possess)— Certainly many attributes could be examined, and many do merit thought on the part of the individual goal setter. Such an inquiry, however, is beyond the scope of this book. Yet, there are two attributes that are directly related and consequently are discussed here.

First, "similar goals." Working for commonly sought goals provides husband and wife with a basic rationale for their relationship. These mutual desires (goals) help to increase the compatibility between husband and wife, thus enhancing the possibility of a lasting relationship.

Conflicting goals are the cause of much marital strife. Yet, unfortunately, it is not unusual for a couple to marry even though their objectives for the future are dissimilar. Generally, marriages are formed as a result of a physical attraction and/or common

---

* The asterisk denotes "no further comment."

interests at a point in time. However, people have some sort of goals for the future, even though they be vague. Because of this vagueness—in the minds of both husband and wife—it is possible that they really do not understand what the other is trying to achieve. Only after a period of time does it become apparent to the couple that their goals are divergent. Then, as is often the case, the partners decide that divorce is the most satisfactory solution.

The second attribute to be mentioned here is "similar background." Let us assume that a husband and wife do have similar goals. Still, these goals must be made operational. People with similar frames of reference will, generally speaking, see similar ways to achieve given goals. And the converse is also true. Consequently, a husband and wife with widely disparate backgrounds will have difficulty in agreeing on common means of attaining given goals, or, in fact, may not even be cognizant that their goals are similar.

This does not mean to imply that people with differing backgrounds should not marry, but if your intended spouse does come from a widely different background, this could become a severe source of conflict.

*Marriage* (Time Together)—At the beginning of this chapter (see *Occupational Goals, Travel* [Away from Home] page 40), it was noted that at certain periods during a marriage, it may be necessary for the husband to be at home more times than others.

Not to refute the above point—but rather to add another dimension to the goal—consider this: How you spend your time with your spouse will probably be much more important than the quantity of time. Several evenings a month with your spouse doing things together that provide both of you with great enjoyment may be more important than twenty to thirty evenings spent together in semi-boredom.

*Marriage* (Communication)—For many reasons it is important that husband and wife be able *really* to communicate with each other. (Communication should not be confused with what has been termed "duolog"—one person talking, but the other not listening.) Two of the major reasons have already been mentioned: first, to make sure that you and your spouse communicate to each other your goals so that you will be working toward similar (or at least compatible) goals; second, to communicate the plans for achieving these goals, so that both of you can see how your daily actions are leading toward their achievement.

Another important reason for real communication is what might be classified as "environmental disparity." Quite often the husband is in one type of environment, the wife in another. Each is being changed—remolded—by these different environmental forces. The intensity and direction of the change vectors may be quite dissimilar, and, over a period of time, the husband and wife may develop entirely separate and different goals and plans for the future.

Communication can help avoid the above dangers, but this communication must be *real* and significant. It must be something more than just casual banter. If you want a lasting marriage relationship, it would seem that at least Type 2 communication is a must.

*Marriage* (Sexual Adjustment)—The term "sexual adjustment" could mean that you, as goal setter, determine to adapt a mutually satisfying relationship with your partner. However, if you have particular basic patterns of sexual behavior that are necessary to your well-being, it would be important to establish these criteria. Choosing a partner who would be capable of offering satisfaction within these limits could save you a great deal of frustration and could facilitate the realization of your goals.

*Marriage* (Social Life)*

*Marriage* (Children)*

*Parent-Child Relationship* (Attributes You Feel Your Children Must Possess)—If you have circled some of these qualities, then plan to start development of these traits in your child(ren) at an

---

* The asterisk denotes "no further comment."

early age. Do not wait until he (or she) is ready for school. More and more scientific evidence is being accumulated showing the importance of the first few years of a child's life.

*Parent-Child Relationship* (Time Together)—Note: see *Marriage* (Time Together), page 79.

*Parent-Child Relationship* (Communication)—Note: see *Marriage* (Communication), page 79.

*Close Relationships With Relatives* (Other Than Spouse or Children) *and/or Friends**

*Participation in Community Affairs**

*Social Life**

*      *      *

The next step is to check your goals to see if they are operational. First, examine your income and capital requirements in relation to your anticipated income and capital accumulation.

*Income and Capital Requirements—*
*Availability Reconciliation*

Examine the chart on pages 82 and 83. (If you are using a library book, reproduce the chart.)

Below is a guide to help you complete the chart. Note: You will probably find it necessary to refer to your Must-Goal Lists while filling in the chart.

    *a. Savings:* Place in the appropriate income-requirement columns how much you will need to save per annum in order to meet your savings requirements.

    *b. Home Costs:* Here are some rough approximations of the current expenditures and capital requirements for home ownership:

        1. You will need a minimum down payment of 20 percent of the purchase price.

---

* The asterisk denotes "no further comment."

2. Assuming a 25-year, 7½ percent mortgage, the monthly payments will be approximately $7.39 per $1,000 on the unpaid balance. This includes interest and principal.
3. Although real estate taxes vary from state to state and township to township, figure $2.00 per $1,000 on the market value of the house.
4. Insurance costs and utilities differ widely from company to company, from area to area, and from home to home. Furthermore, there is not a linear relationship between home value and the cost of insurance and utilities. Rough estimates are, however, as follows: $20,000 home, $40.00 a month; $50,000 home, $70.00 a month.

Five examples are presented below to give a better idea of home costs:

| Market Value | $15,000 | $20,000 | $30,000 | $40,000 | $50,000 |
|---|---|---|---|---|---|
| Minimum Down Payment | 3,000 | 4,000 | 6,000 | 8,000 | 10,000 |
| Balance | 12,000 | 16,000 | 24,000 | 32,000 | 40,000 |
| Monthly Payments Interest and Principal (assuming a minimum balance) | 89.00 | 118.00 | 177.00 | 236.00 | 295.00 |
| Taxes | 30.00 | 40.00 | 60.00 | 80.00 | 100.00 |
| Insurance | 4.00 | 6.00 | 8.00 | 10.00 | 12.00 |
| Utilities | 25.00 | 40.00 | 50.00 | 60.00 | 70.00 |
|  | 148.00 | 204.00 | 295.00 | 386.00 | 477.00 |
| Yearly Payments | $1,776.00 | $2,448.00 | $3,540.00 | $4,632.00 | $5,724.00 |

c. *Apartment or House Rental:* If appropriate, enter annual rental here.
d. *Vacation Home Costs:* To determine the cost of ownership of a vacation home, generally speaking, the same structure as above may be used. The major variations would be taxes and utilities.
e. *Life Insurance:* Rates vary widely, depending upon the age and health of the insured, the company, and the type of

INCOME AND CAPITAL REQUIREMENTS—AVAILABILITY ANALYSIS

| | 1st Interim Target Date | | 2nd Interim Target Date | | Planning Horizon | |
|---|---|---|---|---|---|---|
| | Income Requirements | Capital Requirements | Income Requirements | Capital Requirements | Income Requirements | Capital Requirements |
| a. Savings, etc. | | | | | | |
| b. Home | | | | | | |
| c. Apartment Rental | | | | | | |
| d. Vacation Home Costs | | | | | | |
| e. Life Insurance Costs | | | | | | |
| f. Other | | | | | | |
| Other | | | | | | |
| Other | | | | | | |
| Other | | | | | | |
| g. Social Life | | | | | | |

| h. Vacations | i. Hobbies | j. Other Expenses | k. Total Income Requirements | l. Total Capital Requirements | m. Must-Goal Annual Salary | n. Anticipated Income from Other Sources | o. Net Income (m + n) | p. Income Surplus or Deficit (o - l) | q. Capital Available | r. Capital Surplus or Deficit (q - l) |
|---|---|---|---|---|---|---|---|---|---|---|
| | | | | | | | | | | |

program. A rough estimate on a straight life policy, however, is $20 per $1,000.

f. *Other:* If you had "Other" Must-Goals (see page 57), fill
in the appropriate columns.

g. *Social Life:* Estimate the annual cost. Here is an example of
the Must-Goal—Social Life Type 1 (see page 47) for the
planning horizon. You plan to entertain a few friends in
your home twice a month, to go out to dinner only occasionally, and to limit club or lodge dues and expenses to
something under $150. The expenses can be anticipated as
follows:

> 24 social evenings at home @ $1.00 per
> person    = $192.00
> 6 evenings out per year @ $12.00    =    72.00
> Club or lodge expenses    =    150.00
>                                        $414.00

If, on the other hand, you chose the Must Goal—Social
Life Type 3 (see page 47), your expenses might be
sharply higher. Interpreting this to mean three evenings out
a month and membership in a good country club, the expenses were determined as follows:

> 36 evenings out per year @ $30.00    = $1,080
> Club dues and miscellaneous expenses
> associated with the club    =    850
>                                        $1,930

In addition, $2,500 of capital was needed for initiation fees
and/or bond for membership in the country club.

h. *Vacations:* Enter annual costs.

i. *Hobbies:* Enter annual costs.

j. *Other Major Expenses*—food, clothing, etc. Although you
may not have considered these as Must Goals, you still must
take them into consideration in determining income requirements.

Again, although costs vary widely, depending on income,
personal tastes, and size of the family, on the next page are

| | Expenditures for MEI Family of Four by Income Level (in thousands) | | | | | | | All Size MEI Families Consensus |
| --- | --- | --- | --- | --- | --- | --- | --- | --- |
| | Under $20 | $20–25 | $25–30 | $30–37.5 | $37.5–50 | $50+ | Consensus | |
| Food | 13% | 12% | 10% | 9% | 7% | 5% | 9% | 9% |
| Housing | 26 | 23 | 19 | 22 | 12 | 17 | 20 | 20 |
| Apparel | 4 | 6 | 5 | 5 | 4 | 4 | 5 | 5 |
| Transportation | 11 | 9 | 9 | 9 | 8 | 7 | 9 | 9 |
| Education | 4 | 4 | 5 | 7 | 7 | 11 | 6 | 5 |
| Health | 4 | 3 | 3 | 3 | 2 | 2 | 3 | 3 |
| Recreation | 7 | 7 | 6 | 5 | 5 | 7 | 6 | 6 |
| Life Insurance | 2 | 3 | 3 | 4 | 4 | 2 | 3 | 3 |
| Savings | 6 | 9 | 10 | 10 | 17 | 10 | 10 | 11 |
| Miscellaneous | 10 | 7 | 10 | 7 | 10 | 3 | 8 | 8 |
| Tax | 13 | 17 | 20 | 19 | 24 | 32 | 21 | 21 |
| | 100% | 100% | 100% | 100% | 100% | 100% | 100% | 100% |

percentage ranges for these other major expenses according to income levels, as estimated by *Business Management* (January 1968).

Note those categories that you have already entered on the "Income and Capital Requirements—Availability Analysis." Determine the approximate annual expenditure for each and enter in the appropriate columns on line *j*.

   *k*. Total your income requirements (a + b . . . j).
   *l*. Total your capital requirements (b + d . . . j).
   *m*. Record your Must Goal Annual Salary (m).
   *n*. Record income you anticipate from other sources (n).
   *o*. Total net income (m + n).
   *p*. Subtract total income requirements (k) from net income (o). This total (p) shows the surplus (or deficit) in annual income requirements.
   *q*. Record capital available at the beginning of the period plus capital accumulated during the period (a).
   *r*. Subtract the capital requirements (l) from capital available (q). This total shows the surplus (or deficit) in annual capital requirements.

If, after this analysis, you find that you have a surplus of income available and capital accumulated, you are ready to proceed. If you have a deficit, however, it will be necessary for you to make some adjustments. It is recommended that you first reexamine your income and/or capital requirements. Ask yourself, "Are all of these expenditures necessary?" It may be that you will be able to pare down some of the income and/or capital requirements. If not, then raise your income requirements.

*Time Requirements Reconciliation*
Although it is still premature to consider making plans, it is

still a good idea to check time requirements to see if your goals seem within the limits of operational feasibility.

Reexamine your Must-Goal Lists, especially the following categories:

*Travel* (Away from Home)
*Physical Fitness*
*Personal Skills*
*Vacations*
*Time With Hobbies*
*Marriage* (Time Together)
*Parent-Child Relationship* (Time Together)
*Close Relationship With Relatives* (Other Than Spouse or Children) *and/or Friends*
*Participation in Community Affairs*
*Social Life*

Note the time requirements for each of these.

At first glance it usually seems that there just is not enough time. However, a person can manage a considerable number of activities by combining them. For example, a father might get his children involved in his hobby. This would enable him to spend time on his hobby as well as being with his children.

If you feel it would be impossible to accomplish all of your stated Must Goals—in spite of whatever correlation you might gain—then carefully examine your Must-Goals Lists. Reestablish your Must Goals in order to compress time requirements so that they seem within the realm of feasibility.

*     *     *

After you have completed the reconciliation, check over your goals again. Make sure that they still represent your desires in life.

You are now ready to proceed to the next chapter. I would suggest, however, that you wait until tomorrow before you start Chapter V.

## *A Look Ahead*
## (*Time Required: 30 minutes*)

Living a full and rewarding life does not "come naturally" to many people. A few are lucky; things just seem to happen for them. But for many—possibly the majority—the better life comes only with well-directed effort.

You are to be congratulated. By establishing specific objectives, you have taken the first step in directing your life toward what is meaningful to you.

Your next steps are to devise plans for the achievement of your goals and, of course, to put these plans into action. Many books have been written suggesting how to prepare a résumé, how to select the right job, how to get ahead on the job, how to find the right mate, how to raise your children, and so forth. It is not the purpose of this chapter to compete with these many and lengthy volumes. Rather, it is designed to offer a basic format for you to follow in developing and implementing plans to achieve your goals.

### *How to Develop Plans*

*Understand Yourself.* The fisrt step is to make sure you are "well acquainted" with yourself so you can concentrate on efforts that will give you the greatest returns.

You have developed certain interests in the past, and you have a "head start" in certain areas. For instance, perhaps

- you have leadership capabilities.
- you have a ready ability to detect feelings of others.

- you are good at persuading others.
- you are a good speaker.
- you are good at research.
- you are a good writer.

It will require less effort on your part if the "road" leading to your goals is not a strange one, but rather one marked with familiar and well-liked landmarks.

Some students already have a pretty good idea of their likes, their dislikes, their strong points, and their weak points; and, in such cases, formal testing may not be necessary. This may be true in your case. However, if you feel that you should have a better understanding of yourself, why not contact your school guidance counseling center? If your school does not have testing facilities, they will be able to direct you to a private guidance center.

You may also contact your State Department of Education (Bureau of Guidance and/or Counseling), which may have such a service or can recommend approved private consultants and clinics in your locality. You may contact the American Personnel Guidance Association in the city nearest you. Finally, you may consult your local telephone book Yellow Pages under "Vocational Guidance."

*Become Familiar With Opportunities.* Once you understand yourself, the next step is to become familiar with the opportunities available to you. Perhaps you already know how you can reach your goals, and these means seem satisfactory to you. Even if this be the case, I would still urge you to consider other alternatives. A basic reason for this suggestion is that by looking at alternatives, you might uncover routes to your goals that are shorter, easier, and even more interesting. So, even if you know how to reach your goals, it will probably be worth your time to consider alternative plans.

Many individuals lack insight as to what plans they should implement in order to reach their goals. Although plenty of opportunities exist, unfortunately they do not know it. Consequently, they continue to pursue activities that will never take them closer to the accomplishment of their goals.

You may be in a similar situation. If so, you will need to acquire information to give you insights as to how your problems may be solved.

If you are one of the many persons who do need additional information, you are probably saying to yourself, "That sounds like a lot of work." If you feel this way, keep this point in mind: The decisions you make *now* concerning your job and your personal and family life will affect you for the next fifty years—indeed, they will influence how you will spend the rest of your life.

*How to Find Information on Available Opportunities*

Below are listed some of the sources you may consult to obtain information necessary for developing your plans.

*Books, Pamphlets, and Magazines.* Reading can be the most efficient way of learning. Do not neglect this method; benefit from reading the research and experiences of others. Plan to visit your library, whether to seek information on vocations or on how to conduct personal activities.

In using the library, you may experience the same difficulty as many others; you may have trouble finding appropriate books and magazines. If so, do not hesitate to ask the librarians for help. Explain what it is you are looking for, and usually the librarian will be able to direct you. Strangely enough, many people give up their library search without ever taking advantage of the free, professional assistance available to them.

Some examples of the types of information you can acquire from libraries are the following:

Perhaps your attending college is dependent upon receiving a scholarship or financial aid. In such a case most libraries have copies of:

Juvenal Angel, *National Register of Scholarships and Fellowships,* New York: World Trade Academy Press, 1964.

Clarence E. Lovejoy, *Lovejoy's Scholarship Guide,* New York: Simon & Schuster, 1964.

Bernard Maxwell, *Financial Aids for Undergraduate Students,* Peoria, Ill.: College Opportunities Unlimited, 1968.

These books provide information on available scholarships and financial aid and how to apply for this assistance.

Or perhaps you might be interested in finding out more about a particular career. If so, there is a good chance your library will have a book describing this career in depth. For example, here is a list of books (mostly on careers) published by one company, Richards Rosen Press, Inc.:

*Careers in Depth Series*
   Your Future . . .
—Accounting
—Advertising
—Aerospace Technology
—Agriculture
—Air Force
—Airline Stewardess
—Architecture
—Army
—Automotive Industry
—Banking
—Beauty Business
—Beauty Culture
—Brother
—Own Business
—Chemical Engineering
—Civil Engineering
—Computer Programming
—Credit Field
—Dental Assisting
—Dentistry
—Dietitian
—Direct Selling
—Electronic Computer Field
—Electronic Engineering
—Elementary School Teaching
—Fashion Design
—Fashion World
—Federal Government

—Food Technology
—Foreign Service
—Forestry
—Geology
—Guidance Counselor
—High Fidelity Industry
—Hospital Administration
—Home Economist
—Hotel Management
—Industrial Engineering
—Insurance
—Interior Design
—International Service
—Jobs Abroad
—Journalism
—Landscape Architecture
—Law Enforcement
—Librarian
—Marines
—Marketing
—Medical Assisting
—Medical Technology
—Merchant Marine
—Meteorology
—Minister
—Model
—Museums
—Music
—NASA
—Naval Architecture

—Navy
—Nuclear Energy Fields
—Nun
—Nursery Industry
—Nursing
—Occupational Therapy
—Oceanography
—Optician
—Optometry
—Personnel Work
—Physics
—Pilot
—Pharmacy
—Photography
—Physician
—Printing
—Public Relations
—Rabbi
—Radiologic Technology
—Real Estate
—Retailing
—School Psychology
—Secretary
—Shorthand Reporter
—Social Work
—Television
—Temporary Office Worker
—Traffic Management
—Translating and Interpreting
—Trucking Industry
—Veterinary Medicine

*Aim High*
*Vocational Guidance Series*
—Air Conditioning & Refrigeration
—Appliance Service
—Automotive Service
—Bakery Industry
—Drafting
—Electronic Technician
—Graphic Design/Art
—Hospital
—Iron and Steel
—Pipe Trades
—Restaurant
—The Textile Industry

—Watchmaking
—Welding

*Personal Guidance/*
*Social Adjustment Series*
—Homeroom Guidance Activities
—For Thinking Teens
—How to Be an Adolescent . . .
   And Survive
—Your Future as a Husband
—Your Future as a Wife
—A Guide to Skin Care
—Dig That Dish
—Teenager and Safe Driving
—Teenager and Speechmaking &
   Debating
—Teenager and V.D.
—Stories for Thinking Teens

*Student Journalist Series*
—The Student Journalist and
   Broadcasting
—Critical Review
—Creative Writing
—Designing the Opinion Pages
—Editing
—Editorial Leadership
—Feature Writing
—Free-Lance Writing
—Interviewing
—Legal and Ethical Issues
—Making Advertising Pay for the
   School Publication
—News Reporting
—Photojournalism
—Proofreader's Manual
—Sports Editing
—Sports Reporting
—Thinking Editorials
—Writing Editorials
—Yearbook
—Junior High Journalism
—Teacher's Workbook for above

*Military Research Series*
—Alert the Fifth Force
—The American Intelligence
   Community

—From Gasbags to Spaceships
—Hallowed Ground
—How to Qualify for the Service
  Academies
—The Infamous Wall of Berlin
—NATO
—Our National Attic
—Pacts for Peace
—Reilly's Battery
—Reserve Officers Training Corps
—Secret Air Missions
—You and the Draft

*The Theatre Student Series*
—Acting
—Complete Production Guide to
  Modern Musical Theatre
—Concert Theatre
—Costuming
—Directing
—Properties and Dressing the Stage
—Scenery
—Scenes to Perform

*Larger Type Editions*
  Your Future in . . .
—Own Business
—Direct Selling
—Elementary School Teaching
—Hotel Management
—Insurance
—Jobs Abroad
—Model
—Optometry
—Personnel Work
—Public Relations
—Retailing
—Aim for a Job in Automotive
  Service
—Aim for a Job in a Hospital
—For Thinking Teens
—How to Be an Adolescent
  And Survive
—Your Future as a Husband
—Your Future as a Wife
—A Guide to Skin Care
—Nursery Industry

Many of these books are appropriate for both high-school and college graduates.

If you are not going on to college, you might be interested in learning about the many jobs that require a high-school diploma or less. Such data, as well as pay scales, can be found in this book:

Charles Adams and Samaria Kimball, *Job Facts,* Reading, Mass.: Addison-Wesley Publishing Co., Inc.

If you want information concerning job opportunities for recent college graduates, one specific source I would recommend is the *College Placement Annual.* As stated in the 1968 issue, this annual describes:

. . . the occupational needs normally anticipated by 2,100 corporate and governmental employers, and is published on a non-profit basis as a service to college and university seniors, graduate students, and alumni. The publication provides data concerning those firms which ordinarily recruit college graduates.

A free copy may be obtained at your college or university placement office, or from the armed services. These sources distribute the publication in cooperation with the publisher.

*Guidance Counselors.* Most high schools and universities have counseling centers to assist students with various problems, ranging in scope from aptitude testing to vocational counseling. These can be excellent sources of information, and if you are fortunate enough to be attending a school that has such a center, I would consult this source first. Usually the advisers are very competent, and the charge is minimal or nonexistent. Some college vocational guidance centers first interview the student to determine what kind of job he is best suited for, considering his goals and his aptitudes and interests. Then they counsel the student as to how to go about getting this kind of job, by helping him prepare a résumé, suggesting various books and pamphlets to read, and even arranging specific job interviews. If your school does not offer such a service, you might contact your State Department of Education to see what kind of counseling services are available, or you might work with a private firm.

If you are seeking information concerning how to plan to meet a personal or family goal, you may wish to contact your pastor, priest, or rabbi. If you would like advice from such a source but have no church affiliation, ask your friends. Perhaps they know of such a person who is particularly good at counseling. Or you can take the liberty of calling any minister, priest, or rabbi. You can be sure he will be glad to help you with your plans.

*Job Interviews.* Quite frequently students have found job interviews an excellent source for gathering background information. If your school has campus interviewing, you may wish to take advantage of this source to find out about various occupations. It is convenient for you, since recruiters come to the campus. Another efficient way to interview a number of firms is to attend programs such as "Operation Native Son" or "S.C.A.N.," which are designed to bring together a large number of employers and applicants. (Note: Sometimes these are designed specifically for college students.) Typically they are held in a center city hotel in a large metropolitan area. The job interviewing sessions are normally held during vacation periods and last for two to three days. There is no—or only a minimal—charge for the students who utilize this opportunity. To find out if there is such a program in your area, call your university or the Chamber of Commerce in a large metropolitan area near you.

*General Hint:* Try to schedule your interviews with firms in various industries—this will widen your prospects.

*Employment Agencies.* Some students have found employment agencies helpful. However, be careful using this source. Unfortunately, personnel counselors at *some* employment agencies are mainly concerned with their commissions and not whether you are placed in a job that will enable you to meet your occupational objectives.

*Friends and Relatives.* You may have friends or relatives who are particularly knowledgeable in certain areas. Do not hesitate to ask them for advice.

*A Note on the Selective Service.* On November 26, 1969 President Nixon signed into law a bill allowing for a Selective Service lottery. Starting in 1970, draftees will be selected on a random basis. Under this new regulation, a person's prime exposure would be during the year of his nineteenth birthday. It would be unlikely that he would be drafted after that year.

Although the bill is a fundamental change, it does not alter the regulations deciding who goes into the pool of draft eligibles subject to the lottery. Deferments will still be granted. However, a person receiving an educational or occupational deferment must undergo a year of eligibility when his deferment expires, just as though he were 19.

There are a considerable number of options open to a young man of draft age. Monro MacCloskey, in *You and the Draft*, emphasizes the importance of careful planning on the part of the individual:[1]

Most young men can expect to have their career plans affected by military service. By proper planning, however, they will effectively serve their country and themselves at the same time. There are more options than ever before, not only between the draft and enlistment, but between different kinds of enlistment with variations between active and reserve service. For example, the services offer many choices as to the type of service, kind of training, overseas duty, and other opportunities which may be selected *before* actually enlisting. These choices deserve careful consideration. The deferment possibilities which permit a student to complete his education should also be examined. The student who fails to plan for his military service before he becomes draft-eligible stands to lose much of his freedom of choice and may very well waste his best opportunity to contribute to his country and to his own future.

*If you are planning to go to college,* you have a number of major alternatives available to you:

One of your choices is to enlist in the regular service immediately after high school. This course of action has three major advantages:

• For the many young men at this age who really do not yet know what they want to be, whether they want to continue their education or take a job, etc., it provides a maturing and broadening experience which better equips them to make these important decisions. Many college educators feel that the young man who has had military experience and then decides to continue his education makes a better and more serious student.[2]

---

[1] Monro MacCloskey, *You and the Draft,* New York: Richards Rosen Press, Inc., 1965, p. 14.

[2] *Ibid.,* p. 15.

- You will be entitled to receive the G.I. Bill after discharge. When you enter college you will receive $130 a month in payments for up to 36 months (assuming you are single and a full-time student).
- If you enlist, you will be given some choice as to the type of work to which you will be assigned, and as to your duty area.

The period of enlistment varies from service to service; however, the minimum is usually no less than three years.

You might decide to enlist after graduation from college. This has the advantage, as mentioned above, of better assignments, but this feature is offset by a longer service-time requirement. Consequently, few graduates enlist in the regular service, unless they do so with the intention of entering an officer candidate school. The following are some definite advantages of serving as a commissioned officer:

- The pay is comparable to starting salaries for college graduates who go into industry.
- An officer is usually placed in a position requiring the use of leadership skills, thus enabling him to develop skills that will be of great use in civilian life.
- An officer is usually placed in a position of responsibility.
- There is some glamour attached to being a commissioned officer.

On the other hand, there are some drawbacks:

- The service time is lengthened.
- A person may be assigned to a task that is of little interest to him.
- There is no guarantee that you will be assigned to a position that will develop those skills required for your civilian career.

Another alternative is to enter college and "wait and see." Under 1969 Selective Service policies, students are deferred until after their college education is completed (baccalaureate degree). It is possible that within the next four years the Selective Service will be replaced by a volunteer army. If such an event should take place, you would not be subject to being drafted by lottery.

A fourth course of action open to you is to enter a Reserve Officer Training Corps while in college. Although specifics may vary from service to service, basically this is the way the Army R.O.T.C. program works: For the first two years, a candidate is required to attend one or two hours of class and participate in a one-hour drill session once a week. In the third and fourth years, he attends three hours of class and one drill period a week. During this time, however, the candidate receives a $50 a month stipend. The candidate is required to attend a six-week summer camp, for which he is paid $290. Upon graduation, he is commissioned a second lieutenant and is obligated to spend two years on active duty.

Still another alternative is to join a reserve unit while in college. This enlistment will allow you to substitute reserve training for two years of continuous active duty. The requirements are as follows:

- Between four and one-half and six months of active duty (a one-time requirement), Private (E-1) pay, $105 a month.
- For six years:
  —One weekend of training every month, Private's (E-1) pay, $13.50.
  —Two weeks of summer camp every year, Private's (E-1) pay, $62.50.

Reserve unit training, although it allows you to train while at home, has the following disadvantages:

- The reserve meetings each month for six years may put a strain on your family life.
- You may have to forgo your vacations for six years because of your summer camp obligations.
- You may be prevented from accepting employment requiring traveling (or relocation). You must attend meetings; if you do not, you will be subject to the Selective Service.

In spite of the disadvantages, most young men find reserve training a very attractive way to fulfill their service obligations. Consequently, in many localities of the country it is very difficult to
find a reserve unit that has an opening (for example, in 1969 one
reserve unit in Philadelphia reported that it had 500 applicants
for four openings). If you should elect this alternative, it is suggested that you apply as early as possible to the unit in which you
would like to serve.

The sixth alternative available is to seek a critical occupation
and stay in this shelter until you are no longer eligible for the
draft. What is termed a "critical occupation" differs from locality
to locality. However, some of the "typical" critical occupations
are:

- Male nurses.
- Some types of agricultural workers.
- Teaching in ghetto schools.
- Tool and die workers.
- Defense work.

A major disadvantage to this shelter is that a person may spend
up to six years in an occupation that may be of little value to
him; he might have better served himself if he had spent the two
years in the service and then entered an occupation that was his
intended life work.

The final choice available is this: If you are going to medical
school, the present draft laws allow you to continue your studies
until completion. After you have received your medical degree,
however, you will be required to serve two years on active duty.
You will be commissioned as a first lieutenant upon entry into
the service. If you have completed your residency before induction you will be commissioned a captain.

If you are not going to college and you are in the high-school
class of '70, '71, or '72, it is unlikely that the draft will be eliminated before you are called to active service. Your basic choices

are to enlist in the regular service, to try to join a reserve unit, to seek occupation in a critical skill, or depend upon your luck. It should be noted that the military service offers many opportunities for the young man who is not college-bound. If you enlist, you may be fortunate enough to learn skills that may be of valuable assistance in your future life's work. Then, too, if you later decide to go on to college or a vocational school, you will be eligible for G.I. Bill benefits, which, in most cases, cover tuition costs and provide a modest stipend besides.

Monro MacCloskey summarizes the advantages and disadvantages of immediate enlistment (for a person not continuing with his formal education):

Arguments for immediate enlistment:
It offers a choice of assignment as to kind and type of training, including technical training and overseas duty assignment.

Arguments against immediate enlistment:
The period of active duty is shorter, which might be of more importance to the individual than the factor that there are no enlistment choices available to the draftee.

By induction time he may have a deferment as a result of having acquired a "critical skill."

He wants or needs to take a job immediately and relies on re-employment rights to guarantee his job on completion of active duty.[1]

In addition to those arguments against immediate enlistment mentioned above, because of the lottery system, a person may not be drafted.

\*          \*          \*

The above are some of the major alternatives available to you. Yet, other choices are open to you under the draft. For specifics on these other choices, I would suggest that you contact a draft counselor. If you do not know of one in your locality, then write the Friends Peace Committee (Quakers), 1520 Race Street, Phil-

---

[1] *Op. cit.,* p. 15.

adelphia, Pa. 19102, for the name of the draft counselor nearest you.

*        *        *

The preceding was not intended to be a comprehensive discussion of alternatives available to you; rather, it was to illustrate that there are a number of courses of action you may take. Since the service obligation is a very important part of your life, you should investigate carefully the alternatives available, and then decide which will enable you to meet your Must Goals.

So that you can base your decisions on accurate information, I suggest that you read the following:

Monro MacCloskey, *You and the Draft,* New York: Richards Rosen Press, Inc., 1965. $3.78. This book describes the student's dilemma, the Selective Service, and devotes a chapter to opportunities available in each of the branches of the service.

Information Kit on Conscientious Objection, Friends Peace Committee (Quakers), 1520 Race Street, Philadelphia, Pa. 19102. $1.50. Included in this kit is a *Handbook for COs,* which contains discussion of how a person may legally avoid service obligation by seeking deferments, as well as one's rights as a conscientious objector.

Arlo Tatum and Joseph Tuchinsky, *Guide to the Draft,* Boston, Mass.: Beacon Press. $1.95. (A copy may be obtained by writing to Friends Peace Committee, 1520 Race Street, Philadelphia, Pa. 19102.) A comprehensive manual on the Selective Service system and how to apply for deferments. Topics include Selective Service rules and practices, draft counseling, how to apply for various deferments, emigration to Canada, etc.

### Make Your Information Meaningful

Too often information is gathered that is not helpful in solving problems. Do not allow yourself to be a victim of this—make sure your information is meaningful.

Below are some suggestions, which, if followed, will help as-

sure you that the time you spend in gathering information will be
well spent.

1. Do not build your plans solely on hunches; base your plans
   as much as possible on factual data. You may be able to get
   a considerable amount of factual information in several
   hours. Why take the risk of basing your plans on false as-
   sumptions?
2. If you seek the advice of another person, be sure to ask
   meaningful questions:
   • Do not be afraid to quiz this person on certain points be-
     cause of possible embarrassment. For example, students
     who feel they must have a large salary early in their ca-
     reer often are reluctant to ask questions concerning how
     to go about achieving this goal. They feel they might be
     ridiculed. Consequently, they may never gain the infor-
     mation they need. If you ever feel this way, ask yourself
     this question, "Which is most important, to find out what
     may affect my life plans or a possible moment of embar-
     rassment?"
3. Since information is helpful only if it is accurate, be sure
   that you check the validity of your sources.
   • Do not take the advice of people who are not really in-
     formed. Too often, people allow themselves to become
     discouraged by others who may be well-meaning but who
     are actually not knowledgeable about the particular situ-
     ation.
   • Does the person giving you the information have any
     reason to distort the truth? If so, verify his statements by
     checking with another source.
   • If the information comes from a published source, what
     is the date of publication? If it is not recent, does it seem
     logical that the information is still accurate?
4. Above all, if you have doubts about the accuracy of any information vital to the success of your life plans, test the validity of this information by checking with other sources.

### Rules to Follow in Selecting Specific Plans

*Generate more than one plan for consideration.* In *Applied Imagination,*[1] Alex Osborn stresses the importance of considering a number of alternatives, rather than just one or two. By so doing, one improves his chances for coming up with a better solution to the problem.

Consider many different alternatives while developing your plans. For instance, build a list of many possible occupations rather than considering only one or two. Delay your judgment on these occupations—do not turn on the red light of criticism—until you have completed a list of, say, ten or twenty possible choices. This will keep the ideas flowing while you are developing your list of plans. Deferred judgment will be particularly helpful if, at the present time, you have pretty well made up your mind as to the "best" way to reach your goals.

*Consider only those plans that will enable you to meet your Must Goals.* The previous step suggested that you generate ten to twenty possible ways to reach your Must Goals. Next, select for further evaluation only those plans that seem to be the best. Carefully study each of these remaining plans, and while doing so, ask yourself, "Will this plan actually enable me to meet the required Must Goal(s) for my planning horizon? For the interim?"

If, for a particular tentative plan, the answer to any of these questions is negative, then check to see if this plan can be modified to provide means for attaining the Must Goal(s) under consideration. If not, discard this tentative plan.

*Caution: Be realistic while evaluating these plans.* Do not merely engage in wishful thinking.

---

[1] People often develop "functional fixation": They "know" how the problem should be solved. They never explore other possible means of accomplishing their objectives and, consequently, overlook better solutions. For further information, see Alex F. Osborn, *Applied Imagination,* New York: Charles Scribner's Sons, 1963, p. 397.

*Determine Want-Goal values.* All of your remaining plans
will enable you to meet your Must-Goal requirements. Now,
determine the relative value of extras that each of the remaining
plans provides. (These are called "Want Goals." For further
information concerning Want Goals, refer back to Chapter II,
pages 27–28.) To do this, study each plan. What are the extras
—over and above the Must Goals each plan will be likely to
provide?

*Evaluate the risk element.* An element of risk is always involved in any plan, but, to be sure, some plans are more risky
than others. Evaluate your plans. Discard any plan that has a
high risk and yet offers a low-value Want-Goal return.

*Strive for synergistic effects.* Some life plans are very efficient
because the component sub-plans complement each other. For
instance, a person wanting, as a Personal Must Goal, to become
an excellent public speaker would achieve greater complementary
—synergistic—effects from pursuing a teaching career than he
would if he chose to become an accountant.

*Coordinate your plans so that all your Must Goals will be
accomplished.* You should not adopt a plan to meet, for example,
your Occupational Must Goals without taking into consideration
its effect on the attainment of your Financial and Personal Must
Goals. For example, Bill H. is a recent college graduate. Let us
assume that he has a job offer that will enable him to meet all of
his Occupational and Financial Must Goals but that requires
extensive travel. Bill, however, has a Personal Must Goal to
spend a great deal of time with his family. If he accepts this
employment, he will find his Personal Must Goal thwarted. As a
result, Bill should turn down this job offer.

To be sure, some plans will be comprehensive enough to cover
several Must Goals. For example, a person may find that by
pursuing the career of a patent attorney he will be able to
achieve all of his Occupational and Financial Must Goals. But

be careful not to select plans to reach some of your Must Goals that will preclude your attaining other of your Must Goals.

### Finalize Your Plans

Now, choose the courses of action you will follow to reach your goals, selecting the plans that meet all your Must Goals and those that offer the most Want Goals, considering risk and synergistic effects.

On the following pages, space (the left-hand column) is provided for you to write in your plans. Again, if you are using a library book, make copies of these pages for your own use.

*Caution:* Make sure you have a plan providing for the attainment of each Must Goal. Your Must Goals are too important to depend upon acquisition by chance.

### Determine Specific Activities That Must Be Accomplished in Conjunction With Your Plans

A study of your comprehensive plans will indicate tasks that you must complete in order to carry out these plans. Your next step, then, is to determine the tasks you must accomplish in conjunction with your comprehensive plans.

Two examples will provide additional clarity.

### Example 1

This person, as his master plan for accomplishment of his Occupational Must Goals, decided to become a patent attorney. He listed this in the left-hand column. In order to carry out this plan, he knew that he would have to earn a law degree and become associated with some firm specializing in patent law. He entered these long-range sub-goals in the middle column. For his short-range sub-goals, there was the problem of admission to law school. He also knew, from his personal inventory and study of law-school requirements, that he would probably have to improve

| COMPREHENSIVE PLANS TO ACHIEVE OCCUPATIONAL MUST GOALS | SPECIFIC ACTIVITIES THAT MUST BE ACCOMPLISHED IN CONJUNCTION WITH COMPREHENSIVE PLANS | |
| --- | --- | --- |
| | Long Range | Short Range |
| *Patent attorney* | *Complete law school*<br><br>*Develop associations with a firm specializing in patent law* | *Enroll in reading improvement course*<br><br>*Search for appropriate law school* |

his reading skills. Possibly his admittance to law school might be contingent upon correcting this weakness. He entered these sub-goals in the right-hand column. (Since it was not necessary that he become associated with a law firm at the present time, he did not list this as a short-range goal.)

*Example 2*

This person decided that becoming a member of the Detective Division of the city Police Department would be the most desirable route for achieving his Occupational Must Goals. Since most police departments require members to have a high-school diploma, he entered this goal under long-range plans. Most state and local police forces operate under the Civil Service system, so plans to take the appropriate test were included on this list.

In the meantime, aware that the Civil-Service exams include a section on mathematics, and since arithmetic was never one of his best subjects, he decided he should develop his skills in this area. He also knew that policemen are required to be in good physical condition. Consequently he planned to develop his physical

| COMPREHENSIVE PLANS TO ACHIEVE OCCUPATIONAL MUST GOALS | SPECIFIC ACTIVITIES THAT MUST BE ACCOMPLISHED IN CONJUNCTION WITH COMPREHENSIVE PLANS | |
| --- | --- | --- |
| | Long Range | Short Range |
| Policeman — Detective Division | Finish high school Take Civil Service test | Build up physical condition maintain good character and reputation Improve mathematical skills |

strength and skills. Then, too, a candidate's character and background are usually investigated thoroughly before he is accepted into the Police Department. This young man, therefore, planned to maintain and build his good reputation. These tasks were necessary for the accomplishment of his comprehensive plans to achieve his Occupational Must Goals. They could, however, be put into effect immediately, so he entered them in the right-hand column.

\*     \*     \*

Once you have completed this step, you are ready to implement your plans with action.

Note: Be sure to list long-range sub-goals that must be completed even though it is not necessary for you to take any definite action at the present time for their accomplishment. By listing these long-range sub-goals, your subconscious mind will be more aware of what needs to be accomplished, and you will unconsciously be generating movement toward the completion of these plans.

| COMPREHENSIVE PLANS TO ACHIEVE OCCUPATIONAL MUST GOALS | SPECIFIC ACTIVITIES THAT MUST BE ACCOMPLISHED IN CONJUNCTION WITH COMPREHENSIVE PLANS | |
|---|---|---|
| | Long Range | Short Range |
| | | |

To be formally reviewed_____, 19____.

| COMPREHENSIVE PLANS TO ACHIEVE OCCUPATIONAL MUST GOALS | SPECIFIC ACTIVITIES THAT MUST BE ACCOMPLISHED IN CONJUNCTION WITH COMPREHENSIVE PLANS | |
| --- | --- | --- |
| | Long Range | Short Range |
| | | |

To be formally reviewed_____, 19____.

| COMPREHENSIVE PLANS TO ACHIEVE OCCUPATIONAL MUST GOALS | SPECIFIC ACTIVITIES THAT MUST BE ACCOMPLISHED IN CONJUNCTION WITH COMPREHENSIVE PLANS | |
| --- | --- | --- |
| | Long Range | Short Range |
| | | |

To be formally reviewed_____, 19____.

| COMPREHENSIVE PLANS TO ACHIEVE OCCUPATIONAL MUST GOALS | SPECIFIC ACTIVITIES THAT MUST BE ACCOMPLISHED IN CONJUNCTION WITH COMPREHENSIVE PLANS | |
| --- | --- | --- |
| | Long Range | Short Range |
| | | |

To be formally reviewed_____, 19____.

*How to Put Your Plans Into Action*

Once you have developed plans, your next step is implementation. Many people do not approach this step in a systematic manner and consequently "bog down" during this critical phase.

Below are suggestions to help you avoid this pitfall and become efficient in the execution of your plans.

*Schedule Your Activities*

Many people have a tendency to put off doing things. Do not allow yourself to fall into this habit pattern.

Schedule your activities on a day-to-day basis. Following is a form that I recommend for scheduling your daily activities. Imagine the top of each daily column as representing the morning hours, the bottom the close of the day. Write in the tasks you are to perform, listing them in the column according to the approximate time of day you think you will do them.

A check list will be found at the bottom of each column. The purpose of these check lists is to remind you that you should be scheduling activities for each of these major goal classifications. Give yourself a check for each of the major goal classifications for which you have scheduled activities. When you have finished scheduling your activities for the week, see how many of these separate categories you have checked. You may find you are neglecting one or more of the major goal categories. If so, try to schedule some activities to make up for these deficiencies.

*Set Aside a Specific Time Each Week for Scheduling*

Do not wait to schedule your activities until you have an "extra" few minutes. If you do, chances are you will never really put your plans into action. Decide right now to spend half an hour every week for formal scheduling. This period preferably should be at the beginning of the week. It should also be a time when your mind is fresh—and when you are free from distractions. Many people find that a time on Sunday works out best.

However, do not restrict scheduling to just your formal planning time. Become "schedule-minded." Throughout the remain-

SCHEDULE FOR THE WEEK OF _____, 19____. (List "Fill-in Activities" in Your Notebook)

| Sunday | Monday | Tuesday | Wednesday | Thursday | Friday | Saturday |
|---|---|---|---|---|---|---|
| Have you scheduled tasks to complete<br><br>Occupational goals?<br><br>Financial goals?<br><br>Self-development goals?<br><br>Family & friends goals? | Have you scheduled tasks to complete<br><br>Occupational goals?<br><br>Financial goals?<br><br>Self-development goals?<br><br>Family & friends goals? | Have you scheduled tasks to complete<br><br>Occupational goals?<br><br>Financial goals?<br><br>Self-development goals?<br><br>Family & friends goals? | Have you scheduled tasks to complete<br><br>Occupational goals?<br><br>Financial goals?<br><br>Self-development goals?<br><br>Family & friends goals? | Have you scheduled tasks to complete<br><br>Occupational goals?<br><br>Financial goals?<br><br>Self-development goals?<br><br>Family & friends goals? | Have you scheduled tasks to complete<br><br>Occupational goals?<br><br>Financial goals?<br><br>Self-development goals?<br><br>Family & friends goals? | Have you scheduled tasks to complete<br><br>Occupational goals?<br><br>Financial goals?<br><br>Self-development goals?<br><br>Family & friends goals? |

der of the week, continually think—and schedule activities. This informal scheduling will enable you to build flexibility into your week, thus allowing you to utilize your time better.

### List Fill-in Activities

As you know, things will happen to prevent rigid adherence to your weekly plans: an appointment will be canceled, you will be "a bit under the weather," and so forth. Consequently, you will find that you are not always able to complete everything you had scheduled; yet often you will have time on your hands— inappropriate to complete scheduled tasks, but still valuable time.

In addition to the activities you have scheduled for the week, you will know of many activities that you will need to accomplish sometime in the immediate future. List these "fill-in" activities in your notebook. Then if you find yourself with some idle moments, check your list and do one of the tasks that is appropriate to the time and the place.

Without such a list, too often we allow ourselves to do something "just to pass the time." You want to avoid this. You want to be living life to the fullest, not "just passing the time."

### Concentrate on Establishing Habits
### That Are Essential to Your Success

For the first few weeks—possibly the first few months—you will have many temptations to "chuck" your plans and revert to your old ways. You will find it difficult to break certain "bad" habits.

You will probably have to change some of your past patterns of behavior in order to complete your plans. Develop new, constructive habits *now*. Blaze new trails, and then be sure to avoid slipping back into your old habits. Force yourself, and soon you will find it easier to do the right thing.

### Be Sure to Put Yourself on the Spot

Here is a tip on how to keep from giving up too soon—tell

your close relatives and friends of your life plans. Put yourself on the spot. By so doing, it will embarrass you to quit. You will be reluctant to give up.

### Commit Your Plans to Memory

After you have established your plans, commit them to memory—just as you did your goals. This will help you to become success-minded; it will help you to develop better habits.

### Learn to Say "No"

Another important reason for committing your plans to memory is this: If you have a clear image of what you need to do to accomplish your goals in life, you will find it easier to say "no" to those events that waste time. You will become more decisive and begin to acquire a peace of mind that comes only to decisive people.

### Seek the "Better" Way

Develop the habit of questioning your activities. First ask yourself, "Is it absolutely necessary that I perform this task?" Then ask yourself, "Is there a faster—more efficient—way I can accomplish this job?" For example, analyze your method of dressing in the morning. You may be following some inefficient procedure that costs you one minute a day. This may seem trivial; however, a close analysis of your other activities may turn up many of these little time wasters, totaling one to two hours a day.

### Tackle Complicated Jobs When Your Energy Level Is Highest

Most people have their highest energy levels at certain times of the day. You may be one of these persons. If so, try to arrange your schedule so that you can tackle your toughest jobs when you are at your best. Take advantage of your spurts of energy.

Do not spend these periods cleaning out your desk or your socks drawer.

Then, too, there may be days when you can accomplish three times as much as on a normal day. If so, borrow some of tomorrow's work. Do not waste precious stamina.

*Do Not Be Afraid of Mistakes*

Too many people fail in life because they are afraid to try. Do not let this kind of attitude prevent you from attaining your goals. One management authority noted that the absence of failures indicates that a person is too conservative.[1] Indeed, Ralph Waldo Emerson noted, "All life is an experiment. The more experiments you make the better."

View mistakes as feedback. Consider them as being similar to the sensing system of the "Sidewinder": Mistakes are a sensing system providing information that will help you get back on course.

*Believe in Yourself*

You will find things much easier to do if you have confidence in your abilities. Here are some tips that will help you become more positive in your approach to life.

- Avoid people with negative personalities.
- Choose associates who are positive thinkers.
- Read books and articles that are inspiring and encouraging. (For suggestions, see ChapterVI, *Shoot for the Moon.*)

*Establish Periodic Reviews of Your Goals*

Planning your life will help you to know yourself better. You will better appreciate your own abilities once you are following a systematic procedure for scheduling your time. As a result, goals that seem important to you at the present may not seem

---

[1] Elizabeth Maring, *Management for the Smaller Company,* American Management Association, Inc., 1959, p. 28.

challenging or inspiring several months from now. If you should ever feel this way, it will be necessary for you to establish new goals and replan your life.

But even if you feel your goals are satisfactory, twice a year you should devote at least one hour to reviewing your goals. Look over your Must-Goal List. Ask yourself:

"Are these goals worthy of me?"
"Are these goals the things I really want out of life?"

If you have a negative answer to one or both of these questions, then establish new goals and replan your life. The time required for this planning will have been well spent.

*Do not postpone your review until you "have time."* At the bottom of your Must-Goal Lists you will note:

```
To be formally reviewed _____, 19_____.
```

Right now, enter in these spaces the date six months from now. Plan to make your review on this date.

### Establish Periodic Reviews of Your Life Plans

Some unfortunate event may occur that will require an immediate change in your life plans. You will have no choice. The plans must be changed. Change them. Then, too, you may want to change your goals. This will, in all probability, also require you to change your plans.

On the other hand, perhaps your life plans seem to be working satisfactorily. Nevertheless, it is a good procedure to review these comprehensive plans at least twice a year. At the bottom of the sheets provided for your plans you will note:

```
┌─────────────────────────────────────────────────┐
│                                                 │
│   To be formally reviewed_____, 19___.    │
│                                                 │
└─────────────────────────────────────────────────┘
```

Right now, enter in these spaces the date six months from now. Plan to make your review on this date.

When you review your plans, ask yourself, "Are these plans realistic in terms of the changing world?" To make sure you can give a significant answer to this question, make it a point to keep up-to-date on changes, which may just require that you read trade journals in your field. Do not be shortsighted: Forecast how changes will affect you. Try to read more than one kind of magazine or newspaper. Look for the types of articles that will cause you to think. They will broaden your knowledge, possibly enable you to determine how you might be better prepared to meet the new requirements of tomorrow's world.

### CONCLUSION

You now know, specifically, the things you really want from life. You have a better idea of how to develop and implement plans to achieve these goals. Now it is up to you to construct your life plans and put them into action.

A Chinese proverb, popularized by the late President John F. Kennedy, states, "The longest journey starts with the first step." You have already taken that first step. Continue and you will find your life gaining significance.

No doubt you will encounter many discouraging moments in the future. For this reason it is most important for you to have faith in your abilities. To ensure positive thinking, choose associates who are also positive thinkers. Read books that are morale boosters. Remember, you stand a much better chance of reaching your goals if you direct your thoughts toward success. These thoughts were very eloquently put by one writer.

You can look toward light, or you can look toward darkness. If you look toward light, you will go toward light; if you look toward darkness, that will certainly be the trend of your footsteps. You must always remember, when you find yourself turned in the wrong direction, to stop and say firmly: I can, if I will, go toward the light. I will turn, here and now, and go in that better direction.[1]

[1] David Seabury, *Unmasking Our Minds,* New York: Boni and Liveright, Inc., 1924.

## CHAPTER VI

## Shoot for the Moon

*(For those who answered "Yes" on page 28, Chapter II)*

*Note:* Included in this section are a number of illustrations and examples. These are in smaller type and are supplemental to the text. If you are interested in only a cursory examination of this chapter, skip these sections.

Many students have serious doubts concerning their ability to attain *real* success in life. To themselves they say, "How can I hope to accomplish anything really great? I haven't actually excelled at anything. Besides, I've always been around so many people who could do things so much better than I."

As a result, many believe it foolhardy to set goals for the things they would truly like to have out of life.

Such anxieties are not—repeat, not—adequately founded. Many reasons for this are mentioned below.

### Accomplishments Are Dependent, in Part, Upon Environmental Influences

For most students, assessment of their capabilities is limited to their performance in school. However, this judgment may be biased for many reasons.

Unfavorable environmental influences may have imposed serious limitations on the student.

- Physical factors, such as poor vision, hearing, or chronic illness, may have interfered with the learning process.
- The student may have been motivated to "goof off" or merely "get by" because of peer-group influences.

- The student may have developed psychological blocks to learning because of overzealous or overprotective parents.
- He may have a very limited background of experience because of meager exposure in his family and school experience.
- Many students have failed to develop efficient learning skills. Academic success is virtually impossible without:
  1. The ability to read rapidly and with comprehension.
  2. The ability to outline and to appreciate the outline development of most textbook materials.
  3. The ability to communicate in an orderly and logical sequence both orally and in written materials.

Failure—and conversely, success—in scholarly endeavors may be mainly the result of environmental forces.

This is true not only of academic pursuits; it holds true for all types of activity. *Many people who possess the ability just do not know how to go about achieving success. Their environment has not provided them with the right "know-how"; consequently success eludes them.*

An apocryphal example illustrates this point:

The Bay of Monterey is a beautiful spot just south of San Francisco—a delight to behold. The scenery is breathtaking, and the large number of fishing boats and pelicans in this area add to the quaintness and charm of the spot. Prior to World War II, the fishing boats had a working agreement with the pelicans—the fishing boats fed the pelicans. The pelicans used to wait for the fishing boats to return to the bay and then would fly out to meet them. The fishermen, who had been cleaning the fish on the way in, would throw out the heads and the guts to the circling pelicans. This procedure had been going on for years; consequently, few—indeed, if any—pelicans living in the Bay of Monterey knew how to catch live fish.

But a tragedy occurred that interrupted this way of life. On December 7, 1941, the Japanese attacked Pearl Harbor. Our country was afraid of invasion of the Japanese armies, so all nonessential traffic was curtailed on the western coast. This meant that the fishing fleet could no longer operate. For the pelicans, their source of livelihood had been removed.

The ocean's supply of fish had not been depleted, but the pelicans of Monterey were untrained to catch these fish and were, therefore, starving. Because of the multitude of pelicans in Monterey, a drastic situation developed. Dead pelicans were strewn across Monterey. Finally, the city council decided that action was mandatory. One late evening in the council chambers, someone pointed out that the pelicans were dying, not because they lacked food, but because they didn't know how to catch live fish. He then suggested that the problem could be alleviated by teaching the pelicans the art of catching live fish. But a problem remained that stymied the council members —who was versed enough to teach the pelicans? The answer, at long last: other pelicans. This seemed logical, so they chartered a plane, flew to St. Petersburg, caught 150 pelicans, flew them to Monterey, and released them. The pelicans of Monterey observed how the others caught fish and got the idea. The problem was solved.

I wonder how many people are immersed in situations similar to that of the pelicans of Monterey? They possess the capability of achievement, yet they don't know how to go about it. Their associations are not with "pelicans" who know how to fish.

A person's environment is favorable—or unfavorable—often because of sheer accident.

Sociologists D. C. Miller and W. H. Form state:

The accident of birth establishes family, race, nationality, social class, residential district, and to a great extent educational and cultural opportunity. This means that the family and its status provide rather definite boundaries within which the new individual will observe the work activities and participate in work life. For some persons, these boundaries enclose wide areas; for others, the scope of observation and experience is squeezed into narrow corridors.[1]

Yet, regardless of the past, it is *now* within the realm of possibility for most students to place themselves in favorable environments, thereby greatly enhancing their odds for attainment of lofty goals.

---

[1] D. C. Miller and W. H. Form, *Industrial Sociology,* New York: Harper & Row Publishers, Inc., 1951.

*Skills Required in School Are Not Necessarily*
*Those Required in Many Occupations*

Another basic reason that assessment of one's capabilities by his performance in school may produce biased results is that the skills required to do well in school are not necessarily those required to succeed in life.

School work, like I.Q. tests, is essentially structured around only a few basic types of intelligence. Yet it is reported that the Aptitudes Research Project at the University of California has perceived over seventy forms of intelligence. A person may lack the ability for great successes in school and still have the ability for high achievement in many career fields. In fact, teachers and professors who are unaware of the many kinds of intelligence are often amazed at the eventual success of their "below-average" students.

*Methods of Measuring Capabilities Are Crude*

Some students have been informed by counselors—directly or indirectly—that they should not set their goals high. These well-meaning counselors often base their opinions on a person's past accomplishments and/or on the results of vocational and intelligence tests. It has been seen how past accomplishments may not be an accurate indication of a person's true capabilities. Despite the fact that there are tests that offer an indication of personal achievement, their validity remains questionable.

An illustration is the case of Fred V. His record in grade school and high school was below average. One of his high-school advisers told him that under no circumstances should he consider entering college. He should take up a trade because his I.Q. tests and high-school work clearly indicated he did not have the capacity for college work.

Fred did not have an opportunity to enter into a trade immediately after graduation from high school, because he was serving in the Army during the Korean war. While in the service, he realized that if he were to live the life that he would really like to live, he would have to further his education. Fred decided that he would go to college in spite of what his high-school advisers had told him.

He had some difficulty finding a school that would accept him, but he was finally matriculated into a small college in the Midwest. Fred managed to get by the first year. However, he said, he worked hard and by the time he graduated, he had a "B" average. Fred was enthused about education and decided he would do graduate work. He was admitted into a graduate school of business administration and, within eighteen months, received his M.B.A., doing almost straight "A" work. Today Fred is a district sales manager for a company that manufactures scientific equipment. He has several salesmen working under him—all college graduates—and is doing well in a very competitive job. He is full of energy, life, and enthusiasm; he is a young sales executive on his way up.

The above illustration implies this: Too often people allow themselves to become discouraged by another's opinion of their capabilities. The advice of these people is often well-meaning, but how sure are they of *our* potential?

Advocates of present testing methods argue that in *most* instances testing seems to have worked out quite satisfactorily (the above case would be classified as an exception). Such results may be acceptable if you are interested in large numbers *only*. But you and I—we are deeply concerned with small numbers of people: ourselves, our children, and our friends. And at the individual level the results may or may not be accurate.

## Attitudes May Be More Important Than Facts in Determining Accomplishments

Many people fail to attain a high level of achievement because of a poor mental attitude. A person's attitude toward himself is vitally important—possibly more important than degrees of innate abilities—in determining his chances for success.

Many authorities, including the noted psychiatrist Dr. Karl Menninger, have agreed that what affects an individual most deeply is not the actual physical surroundings of his life, but the mental view he has of himself.

Experiments with persons under deep hypnosis have provided many insights into how mental attitudes have overshadowed the factual environment.

Hypnosis is, fundamentally, a technique whereby greatly intensified suggestions to the self may result in mental or physical changes. For example, under hypnosis a person can greatly increase his weight-lifting ability if he is given the proper positive suggestion. On the other hand, a professional weight lifter may be unable to lift some light object—like a paper clip—because of the negative hypnotic suggestion.

The famed plastic surgeon Dr. Maxwell Maltz reports how the mind can affect the chemistry of the body. "Tell a hypotized subject that your finger is a red hot poker and he will not only grimace with pain at your touch, but his cardiovascular and lymphatic systems will react just as if your finger were a red hot poker and produce inflammation and perhaps a blister on the skin." [1]

It should be noted that mental attitude can work both ways: for success or failure. If one approaches his problems with the attitude of "can do," then one becomes hypnotized to success.

Regrettably, many people have an attitude of "can't do," and this attitude may be attributed, at least in part, to our educational system itself. A leading educator, Dr. Jean D. Grambs, an Associate Professor of Education at the University of Maryland, reports, "The schools now do a very effective job of making most children and youth feel inadequate." [2] Throughout the educational process, the vast majority of students are constantly exposed to learning situations in which they see others do things much better and quicker than they can. Consequently, many students are relegated to a position of second-class citizens for perhaps sixteen years: a humiliating experience indeed. Dr. Grambs concludes: "Higher achievement levels could be reached by many more children if for these first five years in school they had massive experiences with success." [3]

Success is dependent upon an attitude of "can do." No doubt nature imposes some sort of limits on us, but our capabilities are

[1] Dr. Maxwell Maltz, *Psycho-Cybernetics*, Pocket-Books, Inc.: New York, 1966, p. 29.

[2] Jean D. Grambs, "Achieving Adequacy Through Education," *The National Elementary Principal*, XLIV, No. 2, Nov., 1964.

[3] *Ibid.*

limited or enhanced by our mental attitude. For many people the lack of high achievement has been caused by an improper mental attitude. However, for a given individual, the future need not follow the same pattern as the past. Everyone has within him the opportunity to increase greatly his odds for success by improving his mental attitude.

If you would like to refer to some sources that discuss how to develop a positive mental attitude, I suggest the following:

Ralph Waldo Emerson. Essay on "Self-Reliance." To be found in almost any anthology of United States literature.

Maxwell Maltz, *Psycho-Cybernetics,* New York: Pocket-Books, Inc., 1966. Price $1.00.

Norman Vincent Peale, *The Power of Positive Thinking,* Westwood, N.J.: Fleming H. Revell Co. Price $.75.

*Implications*

The preceding sections have shown the difficulty involved in judging a person's innate capabilities.

It is not meant to ignore the significance of innate capabilities. Some people do learn more quickly than others, and some do seem to have a greater natural ability to do certain types of things. As the late President Kennedy once said, "Life is unfair."

However, just because life *is* unfair, just because some things *do* come easier to some people than to others, this does not prevent those "less naturally endowed" from achieving great things in life. Many routes may be followed to success. Then too, we know little about the capabilities of the mind. Hypnosis, however, gives insight into the phenomenal conquests of an individual who has a positive attitude. And a positive attitude can be acquired.

Great achievements are within your realm. It is not a new idea. Over a hundred years ago Ralph Waldo Emerson said it very eloquently:

You cannot hope too much or dare too much. There is at this moment for you an utterance brave and grand as that of the colossal chisel of Phidias, or trowel of the Egyptians, or the pen of Moses or Dante . . .[1]

So why not "shoot for the moon"? After all, you have only a short period of time on this earth—why not spend it working for things that really mean something to you?

There are distinct advantages in striving for significant goals. If you are working toward something, something you *really* want —something big—you will become excited and enthused about your work. A city planner, David Burnham, commanded: "Make no little plans; they have no magic to stir men's blood. Make big plans; aim high in hope and work."

How can anyone be happy when, gnawing within him, there is a deeply embedded desire for something great, but that something great is being denied because of a "realistic" acquiescence? Assume that a person has the intense desire to achieve a certain amount of fame and to travel extensively. But this same person has been engulfed in the belief that these goals are unattainable because he is lacking in ability. Basing his life on this assumption, he sets more "realistic" goals—at a level at which he is actually indifferent to attainment. Will an enthusiastic outlook permeate his life? Never! He would be the type of person you often encounter: dull, lifeless, discouraged, and unenthusiastic.

If you are to become excited about your life, you must be working for something you really want to attain.

Another benefit from setting your goals high is that you will develop dedication to your daily tasks. It is the willingness to work that determines, in part, what kind of person a man will be.

Emerson, in his famous essay, "Self-Reliance," states:

A man is relieved and gay when he has put his heart into his work and done his best; but what he has said or done otherwise shall give him no peace. It is a deliverance which does not deliver. In the attempt his genius deserts him; no muse befriends; no invention, no hope.

---

[1] From the Essay on "Self-Reliance."

On the other hand, if your efforts are for something you know will be "second rate," you will not be willing to put forth the "extra" that might make you great.

Persistence has been termed the major character trait necessary for success.

One person who had the opportunity of studying both Henry Ford and Thomas Edison for an extended period concluded that the quality he felt was responsible for their great achievements—more than any other—was the quality of persistence.

Brooks Atkinson, the former New York *Times* drama critic, once said that he felt it was not the degree of native talent that was so different among men, but rather the "driving force" of creativity.

It has been said that success is often just one turn away; yet so many people refuse to give it that little extra twist. One develops this necessary persistence by working toward something he really wants to achieve. He is willing to encounter momentary failures, because tomorrow he may achieve what he always wanted.

In summary, personal goals should be determined by what a person truly wants.

It is saddening to think of the people who go through life with their goals set too low for them to get what they would really like out of life. With their goals set low, they rob themselves of much enthusiasm, dedication, and persistence. As a result, they approach their tasks unenthusiastically, half-heartedly, and are ready to quit at the first degree of difficulty. How much can they achieve?

How high should you set your goals?  "Make no little plans . . . make big plans; aim high in hope and work."